The Great ATOMIC NIGHTMARE!

(The Saddest Story in World History!)

By
The Great White Bald Eagle!

Book 099 ♦

(The Cover Photo shows an Atomic Bomb Mushroom Cloud behind the Statue of Liberty, in New York City.)

Copyright, Dedication and Introduction

By the Honest Observer and Chief Agitator!

ISBN — 979-8643-0236-30

00-01 [_] This Inspired Book is COPYRIGHTED 2020 by **The Great White Bald Eagle!** All Rights are Reserved for the Truth's Sake, whatever that might be — since no one seems to Know for Sure with a Capital K nor S: beCause, nothing has been Proven for Sure in any Courtroom concerning any Number of Important Subjects, which are Addressed by **The Great White Bald Eagle,** which is an Obvious PEN NAME of an Inspired Author, who does not Wish to be Identified, and for Various Good Reasons, which will be Clear to all Readers by the Time that they Finish Reading this Wonderful Book, which Reveals HOW TO PREVENT any Great Atomic Nightmares, if anyone is Interested in **"Guaranteed Solutions!" (HOW to Solve our Local and Global Problems in the Most-Rational Manner Possible!) By The Worldwide People's Revolution!®** Book 080, which is not nearly as Popular as: **"Modern Deceived SLAVES!" (10 Simple Steps for Liberating ALL Modern Slaves, Worldwide, Including Yourself!) By Liberty and Justice for ALL!** Book 113, which is perhaps one of the Top 10 Books ever Written, which contains more than 70 Colored Photographs with Astounding Explanations for Wise People to Study with Honest Open Minds. †§‡

00-02 [_] This Inspired Book is now DEDICATED to whomever Desires to Escape from the Great Atomic Nightmare.

00-03 [_] {NOTE: There are Missing Feathers in the Tale of the Great White Bald Eagle. Sorry.}

00-04 [_] No Portion of this Extremely Good Book shall be Reproduced by any Means for Sale without Written Permission from **The Worldwide People's Revolution!®**, which is Responsible for CRASHING the Great False Economy, according to certain Critics, who Conveniently Forgot to Mention that it is Impossible to Destroy Provable Truths; but, it is relatively easy to Destroy a House of Lies, even with only one Tiny Lit MATCH Stick — and especially when Gasoline and Diesel have been Spread all over and throughout the Wooden, Firetrap Mouse-infested Cockroach Den that some Ignorant Fool might call

"Home" — such as those Worthless Houses that Burned Down in Paradise, Californicate: beCause none of those People Discovered the hundreds of Mountains of ROCKS that were Begging them to Use those Rocks WISELY, whereby no such House Fires could have Occurred, and Especially if they were Built like the Pantheon in Rome, which is more than 1,800 Years Old, which has not Suffered with any Heating nor Cooling Bills, much less, any Property Taxes, ElecTrickery Bills, nor Needless Fire Insurance Bills: beCause of being Constructed by a True KING, even as all Houses could be Constructed, nowadays: beCause we have all Kinds of Mechanical SLAVES that would be Happy to Do the Difficult WORK, and not even Mention the Low Wages, which would Naturally be ZERO: beCause Machines do not Care about any Wages, nor do the Mountains of Rocks Object to being Used WISELY. In Fact, that is WHY that the Great Creator God MADE all such Mountains of Rocks, just in case some Ignorant Fool has not Heard about God and his Great Creations, which are very Marvelous to anyone who takes the Time to STUDY those Creations with an Honest, Open and Sound Mind.
‡

Before

After

00-05 [_] So, Stop and Study the *Before* and *After* Photographs on Page 3. (Perhaps you should put on your Sunglasses beforehand, just to make Sure that you do not have your Eyeballs Burned Out by the Bright Shining Light of Provable TRUTHS, which is Obviously what Happened to the Politicians in Washington, on the Capitol Dunghill, who have yet to Notice those hundreds of thousands of Mountains of ROCKS that God Provided for us to Work with, with Heavy Equipment and Beneficial Tools — such as Electric Trains, Rock Cutting Machines, and Rock Polishing Machines, which do not Cost one-millionth as much as Jet Bombers, Submarines, Aircraft Carriers, nor HUGE Trumpite Towers!)

00-06 [_] The Shrine of Immaculate Conceptions in Washington, District of Chief Criminals, is the Perfect Example of what can be Done with ROCKS, and not only for Churches; but, also for Houses, which should be FIREPROOF, Hail-proof, Tornado-proof, Hurricane-proof, Rot-proof, Paint-proof, Termite-proof, Mouse-proof, and INSURANCE-PROOF: beCause that is the Nature of **Beautiful Swanky Stone Dome Home COMPLEXES,** which are Designed by Architects with Riit Minds, who have no Interest in making anyone into an Eternal Insurance SLAVE for a Wooden / Plastic Firetrap Mouse-infested Cockroach Den, called "the average American home," which is Designed by Fools for Fools, who hardly have the Brains of a Jackrabbit, who at least Knows the VALUE of a GOOD SECURE UNDERGROUND STONE DOME HOME, which has no less than 25 Advantages over a Normal American

DISASTER, which can Burn Up into the Nostrils of God by Means of just one Tiny MATCH! Yes, the Highly Toxic SMOKE Ascends Up to HEAVEN, in Great Billowing BLACK CLOUDS of Capitalistic STINK, where it Collects with other Manmade Pollutants for the Holy Angels to Breathe — that is, IF any such Angels are still hanging around up there, which is Questionable. I have my Doubts. Perhaps you do, also. §‡

00-07 [_] Nevertheless, in the Real World of the Living Hell that we have "Created" for ourselves, there are all Kinds of Objections that are seldom if ever Addressed by the CONgressmen in Washington, who are Seldom in their Chambers: beCause they spend most of their Time on their Spiritual Knees with their Telephones, begging for X-number of Dollars for the next Election Deception Campaign, whereby they might get Elected to Sit in some of those Seats in the Senate, or in the House of Fake Representatives, who "Work" for an Average of 1,206 Hours per Year, and Collect more than 180,000 Dollars for their "Services," not Counting the Extra Money that they are Given to Cover Expenses — such as Transportation, Medical Care, Security Guards, and Retirement Pay. Meanwhile, the Normal American Tax Slave is supposed to Enjoy his or her FREEDOM, which is Guaranteed by having a STRONG Military, which Failed to Defend America during September 11th, 2001, when President George Warmonger Bush and Little Dick Chicanery Orchestrated that False Flag Operation with the Help of Donald Rummyfell and General Air Force Commander Cover-up: beCause they Wanted a "Good Excuse" for going to WAR in Iraq, whereby they might Unconscientiously put Trillions of Dollars into the Bank Accounts of Rich Edomites on Wall Street, including Weapons Manufacturers, Chemical Corporations, Medical Snakes, and all Kinds and Colors of Capitalists, who will Say and Do almost anything for Ungodly GAIN: beCause of their *Love for MONEY:* beCause *that* is the Name of the Money Game! Yes, those Hateful Wars are very Profitable for certain Rich People; but, not for the Poor Deceived "GRUNTS" on the Front Line, who have been Repeatedly Indoctrinated with Capitalist LIES — such as, "You are Fighting for our Freedoms!" Yes, it is somewhat Like the Billionaire Insurance Companies in California, who were Fighting for Secure Houses in Paradise, Californicate, who Failed to Discover any of those Mountains of Rocks for Constructing GOOD Secure Houses! †§‡

00-08 [_] O Honest Observer and Chief Agitator, are you Suggesting that we Americans do not Live in "the Greatest Nation on the Whole Earth," which is only 150 Trillion Dollars in DEBT? Surely you must be an Anti-

American Lazy HOG, who Lives on Welfare Checks, and does not even Thank Uncle Sam for it? Moreover, the Great White Bald Eagle must also be Related to a VULTURE, Buzzard, War Hawk, or Screech Owl: beCause no True Red-Blooded American would Speak EVIL of our Holy Government in Washington, District of True Christians. †§‡§§

00-09 [_] Well, my Sarcastic Friend, if those Politicians were GOOD People, no one would be Speaking Evil of them, even though I did Hear some Professing "Christians" using Christ's Name in Vain, not long ago; and I Asked them, "Why do you Dishonor the Name of the Most-Righteous Man who ever Lived, according to the *Holy Bible,* which is most likely an Edomite Construction?" And they said, "What are you Saying? Who are the Edomites?" And I said, "What Grade in the Public School of Ignorant Fools did you Graduate from?" And they were Immediately Ready to KILL me for Asking that simple Question, as if I had Pulled Out their Grandmothers' Tongues, and Cut them OFF with a Chainsaw! Yes, they were so Self-defensive that I had to RUN for my Life! But, Luckily, when we Turned the Corner, there just Happened to be 2 Policemen Standing there, and one of them Drew Out his Pistol, and Ordered those 3 Thugs to STOP! And they did, reluctantly: beCause they Wanted to KILL me; but, I was Thinking that they would Cheerfully Agree with me, and even Confess that they had Attended a Public School of IGNERUNT FQLZ, whose Teachers are still spelling NOLIJ like the Barbarians do, as in K-N-O-W-L-E-D-G-E, instead of N-O-L-I-J, as any Innocent Honest Person would: beCause that is the Way the Word SOUNDS, which should not Offend anyone, if it is speld Correctly. †§‡

00-10 [_] O Honest Observer and Chief Agitator, I am Wondering if the Great White Bald Eagle is Running for the Presidency: beCause I am Sick and Tired of Voting for one of 2 or 3 or more WRong Political Parties, who have no **"Guaranteed Solutions!"** for anything! In Fact, I am not even going to **"VOTE for The GOAT!" (The New Political Party that has Guaranteed Solutions for our Massive Problems!) By The Worldwide People's Revolution!®** Book 109: beCause that Goat is INVISIBLE! Indeed, he has not even Bought ONE Advertisement on TV: beCause he is not RICH ENOUGH to Do that, whereby he does not stand a Chance of Winning! In Fact, there are most likely a LOT of Men, who would Qualify to Govern us; but, they could never Afford to get into any Campaign Races with: **"MARK TWAIN Races for the PRESIDENCY with a Landslide VICTORY!" (The 2020 Presidential Candidates Desperately Need Some STRONG Undefeatable COMPETITION!) By The Worldwide People's Revolution!®** Book 033B. †§‡§§

† The Dagger is called the Sword of Controversies, which Means that someone Disagrees with the Statement, which might be True or False.

‡ The Double Dagger is called the Double-Edged Sword of Controversies, which Means that the Statement is so Controversial, that it should be Proven at: **"The GREAT Worldwide TELEVISED Court HEARING!" (That Great Meeting of the Most-Intelligent and Well-Educated Minds!) By The Worldwide People's Revolution!® Book 041B.**

§ The Section Symbol Represents Sarcastic Statements. Two such Symbols (§§) Together, means that the Statement is so Sarcastic that it Proves itself to be WRong. For Example, most People do not Like Sarcastic Statements: beCause such Statements Require some Thinking to figure them out, which most People do not Like to Do: beCause they Suffer with Chronic Constipation of their Minds: beCause of Feasting on far too many Lies, which have STUCK in their almost Empty Heads as TRUTHS: beCause they have never Actually Heard any Provable Truths since they were Born, until now, which makes them Doubt any Truths that they might Hear, which they Sincerely Believe must be LIES, even though they cannot Explain WHY. For Example, the "Richest Nation on the Earth" is only 150 Trillion Dollars in Debt, which is what makes it so RICH! Indeed, any Ignorant Fool can easily Understand that. Therefore, let us Pray that not all of the Citizens Follow Uncle Sam's Lead, and get themselves into as many Unpayable Debts. †§‡§§

{FOOTNOTE: If the Letters are too small for you to Comfortably Read, please see the 8.5 by 11-inch Colored or Black and White Editions of this Inspired Book in the Amazon Book Store, which is much easier on the Eyeballs. Thank you. Those Editions are also less Expensive: beCause of having less Pages.}

The MENU on the Table of Contents for a Feast of Satisfying Truths!

{HEADNOTE: This Inspired Book contains about 29,000 Questionable Words of Provable Truths, along with a few Photographs with Explanations. Try not to get Depressed by it. Look UP to God!}

{NOTE: Missing Chapters will be Supplied after the Great Atomic Nightmare, if they are needed.}

— Chapter 01 —

WHO IS the Great White Bald Eagle?

01-01 [_] Well, the Great White Bald Eagle is the Penname of an Inspired Author, who is one of the Best who ever Lived, who Impersonates all Kinds of Creatures and Characters, who do not Dare Expose themselves too much: beCause they are in Danger of being Assassinated for Revealing too many Provable Truths. Moreover, one in less than a Billion People Qualify to be Called an Inspired Author: beCause they get their Information from GOD, by Means of the Holy Spirit, whose still small Voice Speaks to their Hearts and Minds. Otherwise, such Authors would have nothing to Say: beCause they are not Inventors of Novels, nor Fictitious Books of any Kind; but, only of Provable Truths and Great Wisdom, which comes from the Gods, and Particularly from the Most High God, who is the Supreme Ruler of all of the Gods: beCause each World has a God to Govern it, including this World, in spite of the Fact that he is not Obvious to most People, whose Name is YHVH God, YHWH God, or Yohoovu God in Swanky Phonetic English, who is the Heavenly Father of Jesus Christ, who Lives Inside of Jupiter, while Jesus Christ Livz Inside of this Hollow Earth, from which the Moon was Born, which Provided the Perfect Place for another Paradise to be Created, which is True for most of the Planets, which are Hollow: beCause they were left that Way after their Moons were Born from them. Indeed, some People find it very Difficult to Believe any such Provable Truths; but, it can all be Proven in a Courtroom with Law and Order, with a Righteous Juj in Charge of it. ‡

Showing results for How many **Planets** have Moons?
Search instead for How many Planests have Moons?

Why would I Want to Search in Google for "Planests"?

How many planets have their own moon?   ⌃

There are about 170 **moons** in **our** Solar System. Most of them are in orbit around the gas giants Jupiter and Saturn. Small **planets** tend to **have** few **moons**: Mars **has** two, Earth **has** one, while Venus and Mercury do not **have any**. Dec 9, 2011

01-02 [_] O Great White Bald Eagle, I See that you have a Loftier View of Life and Death than most of the Birds, who are Philosophers of

Various Kinds and Colors; but, how can we Know for Sure that you are Telling us the Truth about any such Things?

01-03 |_| Well, my Friend, I just finished telling you that Inspired Authors get their Information from GOD, which should be Good Enough for you to Believe me; but, if you Doubt it, just Study the Extremely Good Books of Inspired Authors, and Compare their Words with those of Foolish People with Great Imaginations, who get their Thots and Ideas from Satan, the Devil, which is also True for most of the Zealous Christians, who Seek to Justify Biblical Nonsense — such as the Story of Noah and the Great Flood, which is Based on a Babylonian MYTH, which has no Credibility at all: beCause it was Physically Impossible for a 600-year-old Man and his Family to have Fed and Watered and Cleaned Up after 2 Million or more Animals. But, if you Doubt it, just get yourself 14 American Bisons, 14 Giraffes, 14 Wildebeests, 14 Yaks, 14 Mooses, 14 Reindeers, 14 Caribous, 14 African Water Buffaloes, 14 Indian Water Buffaloes, 14 of each of a thousand Species of Deers, Goats, Antelopes, and Sheeps, whereby you might Prove it — not to Mention the tens of thousands of other Animals, such as Lions, Tigers, Leopards, Bears, Jackals, Hyenas, Foxes, Skunks, Snakes, Rhinos, Hippopotamuses, and a Host of Dinosaurs, while Stocking up all of their Foods in a TINY ARK, plus enough Fresh Water for 14 Months to Water all such Animals! Just one Cow can Drink 40 Gallons of Water during just one Day. I have Personally seen a Horse Drink 5 Buckets of Water within an Hour, and each Bucket held about 4 Gallons. Therefore, just Imagine how much Water that you would Need for Watering 4 Species of Elephants, and 2 of each Kind, who do not particularly Like being Locked Up in Cages for 14 Months, along with a thousand Species of Yacking Monkeys, Squawking Birds, and other Noisy Creatures, who would Drive you Totally INSANE within a Week or less, while Rocking and Rolling around in an ARK! But, you are Welcome to Try it. Just one Disturbed Skunk could Pollute the entire Ark with an Unbearable Odor, which would make you and everyone else say: "Let us get Out of this Evil Place, if it is the Last Thing that we ever Do," as the Song goes; but, not Exactly: beCause the HORRIBLE STINK from the Dung and Piss would KILL YOU! Yes, you could get so few as 20 Dogs and 40 Cats in your own House, right now, and Prove the Impossibility of Living in such a House, if you did not Routinely Clean it up, which could Prove to be a Full-time Occupation for one Person, if you just had 14 American Bisons and 14 Elks, alone, without any Apes nor Kangaroos. Moreover, what Fresh Green Leaves would you be Able to Feed to those Gorillas, Bonobos, Chimpanzees, and Orangutans? What about the 5 Species of Baboons? What would you Feed them? Where would you get the Foods for 30 Species of Rabbits, 19 Species of Coyotes, 12 Species of Skunks, 200 Species of Squirrels, 14 Species of Marmots, 17 Species of Penguins, and 9,000+ other Species of Birds — all of which Eat Different Foods? For Example, would you have any Idea what to Feed a Duckbill Platypus, who might Strike you DEAD with his Poisonous Fang; or what to Feed the 1,240 Species of BATS? Would your Ark have HUGE Walk-in Coolers for Storing Fresh Meats for the Carnivores? If not, how would you keep them from getting SICK and DISEASED? Pandas Liv mostly on Bamboo. Therefore, how many Bamboo Leaves and Bamboo Shoots would you Pack into the Ark? How would you Store it for 14 Months? How would you Remember what each Strange Animal might Want to Eat? There are about 2 Million Species of Ants, which do not Like to be Drowned in Water. What would their Cages look like? Could you Keep them IN their Cages? What would you Feed to them? When would you have Time to Feed them? Could you even Open and Close 2 Million Doors on the Cages during an entire Month? How would you get the million or more Gallons of Fresh Water to all of those Animals during just one Day? Would the Fresh Water be Stored on the Bottom Floor of the Ark, whereby the Livestock might Piss into it? Or, would it be Stored on the Top of the Ark, whereby Gravity might Help you to Water those Countless Beasts, if you had Pipes with Valves? None of the Details are given in the Biblical Account: beCause it was just a Babylonian Fairy Tale, which was Embellished by Lying Conniving Edomites, who Wanted to make a Sellable Book to Gullible Ignorant People with only Half of their Brains Functioning, which can be Proven in a Courtroom! †§‡§§

01-04 [_] O Great White Bald Eagle, the Truth is that there were Millions more Species of Animals at the Time of Noah, than there are Today, and especially of Insects, which do not Like to be Drowned in Water: beCause they Breathe AIR. Therefore, Noah and his Family of Old People could not have Possibly taken Care of so many Creatures, even if Noah had a Magic Pitcher, whereby the Water never Stopped Running: beCause it was Like that Rock that Moses Struck with his Magic Wand, called a Shepherd's Staff. Indeed, not even the Magic Pitcher Theory will Solve the Enormous Problems that Noah would have had within the Ark: beCause of the thousands of Tons of DUNG and PISS that would have Demanded someone to Clean it UP, or else Die with Methane Gas Poisoning, within an Ark that had only one little Window, which Noah kept Closed, lest the Birds and Bats should Escape from such a Hell Hole. †§‡§§

01-05 [_] Well, my Friend, it has been Argued that there was only ONE Specie of Bovine at the Time of Noah, which later Evolved into Musk Oxens, for Example, as well as American Bisons, Water Buffaloes, and so on; but, new Species of Animals is a very Rare Thing to Happen, and does not Happen very Quickly, if it Happens at all. For Example, there are about 160 Breeds of Dogs; but, just ONE Species of them. They can all Interbreed with one another; but, any given Species of Monkeys cannot Interbreed with other Monkeys, Properly, being like Horses and Asses, at the Best, who Produce Mules, which are Sterile. Therefore, for the Noah Story to make any Sense at all, the Ark would have to have been 400 to 500 Times as BIG as it was, just to Contain all of the Animals and their Foods, without any Fresh Water Storage at all. Therefore, my Conclusion is that Lying Conniving Edomites made up the so-called *"Holy Bible,"* just to Sell Books, which we can Prove in a Courtroom: beCause their Descendants are still Doing the very same Thing! Yes, nearly all of the Hollywood Lies are made up by those same Edomites, who are Descendants of ESAU, whom God HATED, according to *Romans 9:13:* beCause God Hates ALL Liars, which Naturally Includes most Politicians, Preachers, Teachers, Professors, Doctors, Lawyers, and JEWS, who like to EXAGGERATE Things, and Stretch the Truth, as they say: beCause it is Done **"For the Love of Money!" (The Strange Things that People Say and Do to Get more Money!) By The Worldwide People's Revolution!® Book 003B.** Yes, it is no Secret that there are Edomites, who Call themselves Jews; but, they are NOT Israelites! {See *Revelation 2:9 and 3:9, King James Version (KJV),* which is Revealing much more than most People might Imagine. I will Tell about them, later on. Just be Patient.}

01-06 [_] O Great White Bald Eagle, most Professing "Christians" are so Ignorant that they do not Know that the Edomites, who are Descendants of Esau, worked their Way into Leadership in Jerusalem by the Time of Christ, who were his Chief Enemies, who Orchestrated his Crucifixion: beCause they were Murderers at Heart, and Jesus told them so, which anyone can Discover by Carefully Reading the little Book of Saint John Zebedee Boanerges, called: *The Gospel of John,* which was written about 100 Years AFTER Jesus was Resurrected, while the Gospels of Matthew, Mark and Luke were written about 160 Years AFTER his Resurrection, and AFTER the Inspired Writings of the Apostle Paul were written, which were the First Christian Writings: beCause the Gospels were mostly Inventions of FAKE Christians, who made up Stories to SELL, which Explains WHY there are NO Original Gospels: beCause there was no Matthew, Mark, Luke, nor John, except in the Mythical Christian Stories, which were Based on Real Life Events, at first; but then, as the Edomites Realized the Potential of Selling Books, they Enhanced those Stories, and came up with a *New Testament,* about 250 Years after Christ. In Fact, there were about 3,000 Manuscripts to Choose from, and they Selected the Best of them, and called them *The New Testament,* which soon became Popular, and Formed the Foundation for Christianity, about 300 AD. Therefore, that Explains WHY the Apostle Paul never Mentioned, nor Quoted anything that Jesus Spoke in any of the Gospels: beCause none of those Gospels had been Written at that Time, including the Book of ACTS, which was Written by Saint LUKE; but, only after Paul was Dead! Moreover, there is much Evidence to Prove what I am Teaching to you, if you Study it Carefully. For Example, in the Gospel of Matthew, it tells about King Herod Ordering the Murders of 2,000 Babies, while Hoping to Kill the Christ-child among them, whom Joseph Rescued by taking the Baby Jesus to Egypt, which Story has no Credibility at all: beCause, according to Roman Records, King Herod was already Dead when Jesus was Born! Moreover, there is no Record of any Census being taken by the Romans during the Time of Jesus' Birth, which is all FICTION. In other Words, the Stories were Constructed by the Edomites LONG AFTER the Events, and some Stories were Fabricated by nothing more than Edomite Imaginations. For Example, there is the Story of Lazarus being Raised from the Dead, which is not Recorded in any Roman History, which would have been a very SENSATIONAL NEWS REPORT, if it had Actually Happened: beCause there were more than a thousand Roman Historians and News Reporters Living at that Time, among whom was Josephus, who wrote Volumes of Books; but, even those Books were Edited and Modified by the Edomites, later on, who Added their Lies to them, which can be Proven in a Courtroom. †§‡

01-07 [_] Well, my Friend, it would be Difficult to say just how much of the so-called *"Holy Bible"* is True; but, I can Assure you that most "Believers" have ZERO Interest in Proving any of it to be True nor False, even as the Muslims have no Interest in Proving the *Holy Koran* to be True nor False: beCause, if it is Proven to be False, their entire False Religious Foundation will be Swept OUT from Under them, leaving them Dumbfounded, Confused, and Extremely Perplexed: beCause they have had Personal Experiences with the Salvation of GOD, including myself! Yes, I was *"born again"* when I was 12 Years Old, whereby I Experienced the Salvation of God through the Forgiveness of Jesus Christ, who Saved me from all of my Sins in a most Dramatic Way, and Changed my Heart and Mind, and made me into a New Creation in Christ, whereby I became a very Zealous "Christian," who even Believed that I would be Raptured Up to Heaven at just any Minute of the Day or

Night! But, behold, some 62-plus Years Later, I am still HERE, just to Fulfill Saint Peter's Prophecy about Scoffers and Mockers arising during the "Last Days," which have yet to Come! Likewise, my Grandfather said that Preachers were Telling those same Religious Lies when he was a little Boy, and they all Died without being Raptured Up to Heaven: beCause it is a Trick of those Lying Conniving Edomites, who made up that Story to keep their Slaves Contented with the *Hope* of going to Heaven when they Die, who are Looking Forward to a Better World, somewhere around Orion or the Pleiades. But, Jesus said, *"Blest are the Meek, Teachable People: beCause they will Inherit the Good Earth, not Heaven: beCause the Earth was Created for Mankind to Inherit and Manage Properly, while the Heavens are Reserved for the Gods."* — *The New MAGNIFIED Version (NMV) of Matthew 5:5,* which Corresponds with: *"May your Holy Kingdom Come to the Good Earth, O Supreme Ruler, and may your Will be Done on the Earth, even as it is now Done in Heavenly Places."* — *The NMV of Matthew 6:10.* {See Amazon dot com usa for: **"The New MAGNIFIED Version of the HOLY KORAN!" (WHY MuhamMAD went to Hell for Spiritual MURDER!) By The Worldwide People's Revolution!®** Book 089.}

01-08 [_] O Great White Bald Eagle, what you Teach makes Perfect Sense, if a Person Thinks about it: beCause it has been Proven in another Inspired Book, called: **"Modern Deceived SLAVES!" (10 Simple Steps for Liberating ALL Modern Slaves, Worldwide, Including Yourself!) By Liberty and Justice for ALL!** Book 113. First of all, the Edomites make us into Education Slaves, whereby we can Obtain their Diplomas, whereby we can Obtain Good-paying Jobs, whereby we can make ourselves into Eternal Work Slaves, Tax Slaves, Insurance Slaves, Home-owner Slaves, Interest Slaves, Mortgage Slaves, Rent Slaves, ElecTrickery Bills Slaves, Food Bills Slaves, Water Bills Slaves, Gas Bills Slaves, Transportation Bills Slaves, Repair Bills Slaves, Telephone Bills Slaves, Internet Bills Slaves, Entertainment Bills Slaves, Childcare Bills Slaves, Drug Bills Slaves, Doctor Bills Slaves, Hospital Bills Slaves, Nursing Home Bills Slaves, and Funeral Home Bills Slaves: beCause we are nothing but SLAVES of an Evil Capitalist Empire, which Pays Slave-labor Wages to most of their Slaves, who barely get by from Paycheck to Paycheck: beCause those Lying Conniving Edomites make Sure that their Slaves have very little Money, whereby they might have some Time to Read Good Books, and Think about Marching against their Slave Masters in Washington, District of Chief Criminals, who do not give a Damn about their SLAVES, except to PRETEND to Care for them, until they get Elected; and then they Conveniently Forget all about the Needs of their Slaves, who Need: 1)

Fresh Clean Air to Breathe, 2) Pure Living Water to Drink, 3) Wholesome Natural Foods to Eat, 4) Natural Clothing to Wear, 5) Secure Stone Dome Homes to Live in, within Beautiful Planned City States, which are Designed for GOOD SELF-DEFENSE: beCause of having TALL STONE WALLS, which have Arcades of Stone Wind Funnels at the Tops of those Walls, for Producing FREE Electricity for everyone, Worldwide: beCause the Tall Stone Walls CATCH the Wind, and Funnel it into the Electric Generators, no matter which Directions the Winds are Blowing from, which is Used Wisely to PUMP the Fresh Pure Living Water from Lower Cisterns UP to Higher Cisterns, which Work as Batteries for Storing Energy, for whenever the Wind is not Blowing, which is Rarely: beCause those Stone TERRACES can be 10 to 60 HIGH, being 60 to 200 feet High in just one Terrace, and as much as 100 Miles LONG, going all of the Way around those **"GLORIOUS Swanky Hotels Castles and Fortresses!" (Beautiful Planned City States for WISE Intelligent Well-Educated People with Common Sense and Good Understanding!) By The Worldwide People's Revolution!®** Book 019B, which just Happen to have more than 5,000 Good Reasons and Great Advantages for Building them and Living within the Borders of them! Yes, it is all Explained in another Inspired Book, called: **"The Right Design for Living!" (A List of Great Advantages for Building Beautiful Planned City States!) By The Worldwide People's Revolution!®** Book 012B. Therefore, Exciting Times are Coming, O Sheeples!

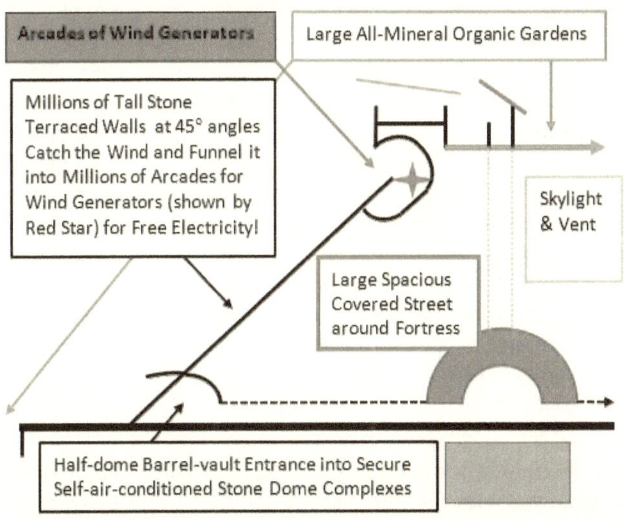

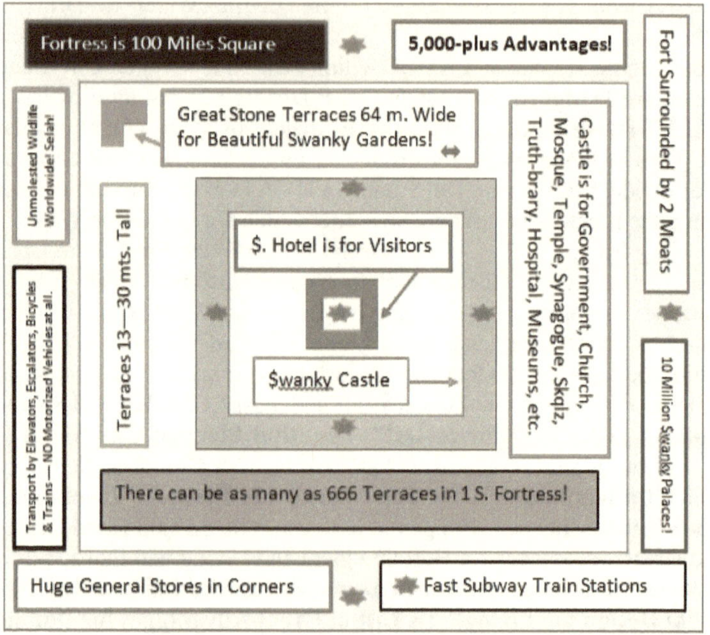

01-09 [_] Well, my Friend, I Challenge any Person on this Good Earth to Think of anything else that has 5,000-plus Good Reasons and Great Advantages for Doing it! For Example, a Car has the Great Advantage of being Able to Transport someone to his Job with Jobe; but, it also has the Great Disadvantage of being Able to KILL a lot of People, while only ONE Person in all of World History has been Killed by an Elevator, and it was his own Fault; and NONE have been Killed by an Underground Electric Swanky Train, which runs behind Solid Stone Walls that are 10 feet THICK: so that not even the Sound of the Train can be Heard, until it comes to a STOP, and the Triple Sliding Glass Doors are Opened Up, which are in Perfect Alignment with the Sliding Glass Doors on the Train, which has Comfortable SPACIOUS Passenger Cars, which are 20 feet Wide and 100 feet Long and 12 feet Tall, with Recliners for Passengers to Rest in, while they Watch Special News Reports about the Wonderful Things that are going on at those **"GLORIOUS Swanky Hotels Castles and Fortresses!"** which are Designed for LIVING, whereby each Family is Set Up Properly for Living, at HOME, who have Large Cisterns for Water Storage, one-acre All-Mineral Organic Gardens, Home-craft Workshops with Well-made Swanky Tools, Sales Shops, Living Room Domes that are 24 to 40 feet in Diameter, plus Kitchen Domes that are 16 to 20 feet in Diameter, plus Walk-in Coolers,

Freezers, Root Cellars, Pantries, and Storage Domes, which are Joined to Spacious Bedroom Domes by Barrel-vault Tunnels, which are 4 to 6 feet Wide and 8 to 12 feet Tall: beCause all of the Doorways are at least 3 to 4 feet Wide; and each of those **"Beautiful Swanky Stone Dome Home COMPLEXES!"** are Covered with LUSCIOUS All-Mineral Organic Gardens: so that your Garden is Directly in FRONT of your House, which is Covering the Roof of the Stone Dome Home Complex below you, in the next Terrace, even as your Roofs are also Covered with Gardens for the Naaberz, who Live above you in the next Terrace going UP: beCause there are 4 to 60 Terraces within any given City State, whereby everyone has a Beautiful VIEW from the Walkways, which go around the Tops of the Terraces. (Study the Drawings just after Verse 01-08.)

01-10 [_] O Great White Bald Eagle, are you Sure that anyone will be Able to AFFORD to BUY any such Billion-dollar Swanky PALACES, which might have 1,000 or more Stone Dome Home COMPLEXES in just one Palace? Indeed, just one Stone Dome Home Complex will Cost no less than 20 Million Dollars for Materials and Labor — unless we Common Slaves suddenly get WISE, and Volunteer to Work for FREE to Build our own Houses; and also Claim our own Mountains of Rocks, for FREE, as well as our own Rivers of Water, Forests, Minerals, Metals, Sunrises, Sunsets, Rains, and whatever else that God has Generously Given to the Edomites, in order that they might SELL all such Things to us Ignorant Fools: beCause of Teaching to us the False OWNERSHIP Doctrine of the Devil, who uses it to make SLAVES of Various Kinds, even as **Liberty and Justice for ALL** has Explained in: **"Modern Deceived SLAVES!" (10 Simple Steps for Liberating ALL Modern Slaves, Worldwide, Including Yourself!)** Book 113. Therefore, when we get our Stone Dome Home Complexes Built, we will just Move into them, Loan-free, Interest-free, Rent-free, Ownership-free, Mortgage-free, and Tax-free: beCause of Establishing a Fatherly Government, which Thinks of us as his Children, who must be Obedient Children, who Learn, Believe, Love and OBEY **"The New MAGNIFIED Version of the 20 Commandments,"** which will Greatly Simplify everything, and Eliminate all Taxes! Therefore, we will put the Bank Robbers into the Trash Can, along with all of the Criminals in Washington, District of Chief Criminals: beCause a RIGHTEOUS Government has no Need for any Banks, nor Taxes at all, which was Proven by **Liberty and Justice for ALL!** In Fact, have you ever Heard of a Father Taxing his own Children for Breaking his Rules? NO, never: beCause all such Children would simply RUN AWAY, and Join the Antelopes! †§‡

{Those African Antelopes have Lived for thousands of Years without any Taxes! So can we.}

— Chapter 02 —

What is the CAUSE for the Great ATOMIC NIGHTMARE?

02-01 [_] O Great White Bald Eagle, what Great Sins have we Committed, whereby God would Judge us to be Worthy of a Great Atomic Nightmare?

02-02 [_] Well, my Friend, what makes you Imagine that GOD has anything to Do with it? Are you one of those Ignorant Fools, who Vainly Imagines that God Micro-manages everything that goes on in this World? For Example, when an Airplane Crashes with Christians, Jews, Muslims, Hindus, and Atheist in the Plane, who all get Killed, do you Think that God got all of them Lined Up for such an Experience? Or, did they get themselves Lined Up for it? I Perceive that you are very Superstitious, my Friend: beCause God had absolutely NOTHING to Do with it; but, the Devil did, which is Confirmed by *the Book of Jobe,* in Chapters 01—03. However, even that is Questionable: beCause it is Suggesting that God and Satan are Playing some Kind of a Power Game with their Guinea Pigs, called Human Beings, who are being Tested by Tormenting them.‡

02-03 [_] O Great White Bald Eagle, the *Holy Bible* leads us to Believe that God does Micro-manage every Detail of our Lives, and especially if we are Believers in him. For Example, President Abraham Lincoln had a 10-year-old Son by the Name of Willy, who got Sick and DIED, whereby God Broke Abe's Poor Old War-Torn Heart: beCause he Loved his Son very much; but, he should have been Loving God very much, instead of Willy: beCause of God going around Killing Innocent Children with his Countless Sicknesses and Diseases: beCause of being an Imaginary God of JUSTICE, who Targets the Innocent Children most of all, who Murders about a Million of them each Year, with Malaria, Starvation, and Viirusez of Various Kinds. {Amazon will not Publish any Book that Mentions the Words "Kuroonu," nor "Viirus": beCause they have Permission from the Federal Government to Limit our Freedum uv Speech and of the Press. Therefore, all Authors have to be very Careful to not Offend Amazon Guidelines, who are very Sensitive, who Search every Book by Means of Computers, Automatically, just in Case someone might Offend her Majesty, if you know what I Mean.}

Indeed, just WHY that anyone would Love such a Crazy God, who Murders so many Babies, is far beyond my Understanding. †§‡

02-04 [_] Well, my Friend, the Problem is not with God; but, with Misunderstanding what is Actually Happening in this World of Woes, most of which has nothing to Do with GOD, who is All that is GOOD, while the Devil Represents All that is EVIL, which is not made very Clear in that so-called *"Holy Bible,"* which contains a LOT of Jewish MYTHS — such as God Micro-managing each Person on this Earth, which does not Fit with Reality: beCause Satan is in Charge of this World of Woes, which has mostly Abandoned the Hebrew God, who was Proven to be Crazy about 3,400 Years Ago, when he Commanded the Israelites to make Genocidal Murderers of themselves by Slaughtering the Canaanites, Hittites, Hivites, Jebusites, GIANTS and other Tribes in the Land of Palestine, which anyone can read about in *First Samuel 15:3, KJV, and Related Scriptures.* For Sure, we can all Understand that the Canaanite Asses and Camels were to Blame for the Itching Butts of the Israelites. Therefore, Slaughter ALL of them, including the Cats and Dogs: beCause they are Guilty! HUMBUG! †§‡§§

02-05 [_] ♦♦♦♦♦ O Great White Bald Eagle, it is Obvious that the Hebrews made up their own Imaginary God, and had him Doing Various Miraculous Things in the *Old Testament,* which never Actually Happened — such as the Israelites Living in Egypt for 430 Years, without leaving a Shred of Evidences to Prove it. For Example, not one Israelite Grave has ever been Discovered in Egypt, anywhere, whose Bones would have DNA to Prove it, as well as the Grave Clothes, and Inscriptions on the Rocks; but, there is ZERO Evidence to Prove any such Things: beCause the Israelites did not Live in Egypt, nor do the so-called "Books of Moses" even Mention the Great Pyramids, the Sphinx, nor anything in Egypt: beCause the "Books of Moses" were Constructed by the Lying Conniving Edomites, when they were Living in Babylon, about 600—400 B.C.: beCause they Wanted to Stabilize their Society by Inventing an Authoritative GOD, with Superior Laws and Regulations, just to Control the Wandering Masses of Lawless People, which every Civilized Society has Done since the Imaginary Tower of Babel, which was Actually a Tower for a Rocket Launcher: beCause they were Building a Tower for a Spaceship Program, whereby they might get Up into the Sky, in Order to Explore other Worlds: beCause they Understood that the Earth had been Populated by the Giants, long before the Creation of Adam from the Elements of the Ground by Jehovah God, who Claimed this Earth as his own Territory, who wanted to Inhabit it with White People, instead of the Black People, who had been brought here by the Giants, in their Spaceships, about 10,000 Years Ago, who Built the Great Pyramids, Jerusalem, Stonehenge, and many other Monumental Sites around the World: beCause those Giants had Great Nolij, who were known, even in the Bible, as *"... Men of Great Renown ..."* in *Genesis 6:4,* which should read like this: *There were Giants on the Earth during those Days, who had come to the Earth by Means of Spaceships, long ago; and also after that, when the Sons of the Most-High God came to this Earth to Inhabit it, and Created Adam and Eve, who were White People, whom the Gods Wanted to Inherit this Earth: beCause the Black Peoples and Brown Peoples had Corrupted it, who were called the Unholy Sons of Unclean Men, whose Dawterz were having Sex Orgies with the Giants for Entertainments: beCause those Giants were Well-Endowed with HUGE Sex Organs, whereby the Unclean Black Men were Swinging between their Spread-out Legs, while Hanging onto their Testicles and Scrotums, whose Testicles were as Big as small Footballs, and their Tally Whackers were as Big as the Trunks of Young Apple Trees. Yes, it was an Evening Sport for them to Play their Games, being Stark Naked, and Well-Oiled, which made them Slippery, which only Added to the Fun of it all, which made the Giants Laugh Loudly: beCause they Really Enjoyed Doing it, and so did the Unholy Dawterz of the Wrongly-conceived Children of Unclean Men, who Loved to Play with their Sex Organs, who Naturally gave Birth to more Giants, even though they were not nearly as BIG as the Original Giants, who came from far-away Worlds in their Giant Spaceships, who were Men of Great Renown and Worldly-Wisdom, who Enjoyed Working with Stones, who Built the Great Pyramids in Egypt, which are Symbolical of the Government of the Gods, which is a Great Pyramid Government, having the Most-High God at the very Top of the Pyramid, who is Symbolized by the Solid Gold Pyramid Cornerstone that is on Top of the Great Pyramid in Egypt, until this very Day, which was there when Adam was Created from the Dust of the Elements of the Ground by Jehovah God and his Chosen Son, who would be Reincarnated into the Body of Adam: beCause he was Appointed to become the Father of this World, and also the Anointed Savior of it: beCause he would be the Beginning of the Creation of Jehovah God in this World, and also the End of its Perfection as the Resurrected Chosen Son of Jehovah God, who would Pay the Price for the Redemption of Mankind from the Fall of Mankind in the Garden of Eden, who was the Holy Angel who Planted the Garden, and Cared for it, along with his Fellow Servants, who were smaller Angels: beCause there are all Kinds of Angels and Gods: beCause each of the Trillions of Worlds Requires a God to Govern it, along with his Holy Angels: beCause it is very Important that only Righteous People and Holy Gods and Holy Angels should Govern the Countless Worlds that are being Created by the Gods: beCause those Worlds would otherwise be Destroyed by Satan and his Unholy Angels and Demon Spirits, who Comprise about one-third of all of the Angels: beCause that many Angels Believed his Lies, who Tawt that everyone should be Forced to be Righteous; but, the Most-High God Tawt that everyone should be Free to Choose to Do Good, and not be Forced to Do Good: beCause that would make them Rebellious. Therefore, all of the Children should be Corrected by their Fathers, whenever they Say and/or Do WRong Things, until they Grow Up, whereby they might make their own Decisions to Say and/or Do whatever is Right or WRong: beCause they should be Free to make all such Choices, whereby they might be Tested for their Goodness or Evilness, whereby they might be brought into Judgment for it. Therefore, the Good Spirits could be Discovered by God's Plan, who Allows Satan to Deceive as many Souls as might Believe his Tale of Lies: beCause God only Wants the Best of Good Spirits to Govern his Countless Worlds, which is Reasonable and Logical, which every Sane Person Agrees with: beCause, who would Want Wicked People Governing them? Therefore, People should be Wise, and Choose the Best of Righteous Men to Govern them, even if they are Giants with Big Chime Bells and Long Soft Cuddly Fat Tally Whackers. However, most of them are not Humble nor Honest: beCause they are very Proud of themselves, which most often Blinds their Spiritual Eyes and Causes them to not See Things Correctly, while also making them Spiritually Deaf, whereby they cannot Hear the Inspired Words of Provable Truths very Clearly, who often Misunderstand all such Words as these: beCause of having Spiritual Ears that are Full of the Wax of Unbelief, you might say. Therefore, the Remedy for that is for every Wise Person to Humble himself by Means of Fasting and Praying for Forgiveness of all Sins, which are Transgressions of the Laws of the Most-High God, who Lives in another Universe, which is a Billion Times as large as this Visible Universe with its Billions of Galaxies, Trillions of Stars and Countless Inhabited Planets: beCause the Good Works of the Most-High God are Endless, who is a Great Spirit Being, whose Name is Keeoojum, who is the Immortal One, who is the SUPREME RULER of all Supreme Rulers in all of the Galaxies, who are called GODS: beCause they are Supreme Rulers, who have Earned their Positions of Authority by the Grace of God, by Choosing to Learn, Believe, Love and Obey the Commandments of the Most-High God, whereby all of the Gods are as ONE, having One Mind, One Spirit, One Opinion, One Understanding, One Purpose, and One Great Goal, which is to MULTIPLY themselves and their Countless Worlds, none of which are just Exactly Alike: beCause each God is Free to Create his own Worlds as he Pleases, even as this World was Created According to the*

Will of the Chosen Son of Yohoovu God, who Lives Inside of Jupiter, who Governs this Solar System: beCause each Solar System Needs a Good God to Govern it. Therefore, each of the Planets must also have the Chosen Sons of God to Govern them, most of which are Inhabited on the Insides of them, including this Good Earth, which is Inhabited by Giants, also: beCause the Giants are more Blest, and especially when they Choose to Love and Obey their Supreme Ruler: beCause they are Bigger and Stronger, being much Bigger and Stronger than African Bull Elephants! Yes, they are Able to Build with very Large Stones, and also Manage their Servants: beCause of being Good Masters. In Fact, in his Glorified State, the Chosen Son of Yohoovu God is also a Great GIANT of a MAN, who will Appear in all of his Naked Glory during the Last Great Day, at the End of the Ages — even as he will Appear to the Apostles Peter, James and John on the Mount called Transfiguration — Riding his Great White Horse, which will also be a Great GIANT, about 600 Feet Tall, with a Tally Whacker as Big as a Redwood Tree! Therefore, let all Midgets Shake and Tremble in his Presence: beCause he will Return with POWER and GREAT GLORY, along with tens of thousands of his Holy Ones, with Flying Spaceships, which are as Swift and Unified as Flocks of Birds in the Sky, which will Move at Lightning Speeds, which the Barbarians will not have Seen before that Time. Indeed, the Dead People, who have Died with True Faith in Jesus Christ, will Arise First; and then those who are still Alive, who Believe in the Anointed Savior enough to Obey him, will be Caught Up into the Sky by Means of Flying Machines, which are Shaped like Saucers, or Big Dishes, whereby one Saucer is Upside Down on Top of another Saucer, which are Managed by Strange Humanoid Creatures with Tiny Tally Whackers and Little Balls: because Sex is of very little Interest to them; but, it is of Great Importance to most People, many of whom are Overstimulated by Bad Diets, which make them Extra Horny and Lustful, who must get Control of themselves by Means of Fasting and Praying, which is the Cure for almost all Physical, Mental, and Spiritual Problems, including Political Insanity; but, not Mislabeled Homosexuality: beCause People are Born that Way, and cannot Change their Natures, even if they Want to; but, they can Control their Lusts, and not Commit Sodomy, which is Anal Sexual Intercourse, which is Forbidden by all of the Gods, some of whom have Frot Sex, which is Man on Man, Face to Face, Penis on Penis, and Balls on Balls, which is Extremely Erotic Sex: beCause of Working the Hands and Bodies in the Right Way, which is why that Jehovah God will be Wrestling Naked all Night with Jacob at the Brook called Penuel (Genesis 32): beCause Yohoovu God is GAY! Yes, he was Born Gay in another World, who Obeyed the Laws of the Most-High God; and therefore, he Inherited his own Solar System, whose Chosen Son to Govern this World is Bisexual, which many Ignorant People will find Difficult to Believe; but, it can be Proven in a Courtroom, if anyone is Interested in it. After all, his Favorite Lover will be Lying in his Bosom at his Last Supper, after Sleeping with him for 3 Years, just for the Proof of it, which is no Sin: beCause Yohoovu God does not Forbid Men to Love one another; but, he Commands them to Love one another, which is the Primary and Most-Important Thing in this Life: beCause, if we cannot or will not Love one another, how can we Inherit any Position in the Holy Kingdom of the Good Gods? Truly, Truly, I say to all of you Humble Honest Men, that God has Created all Beautiful Things to Richly Enjoy, including the Beautiful Bodies of Healthy Young Men, who should Share themselves with one another in a Riit Waa, whereby their Sexual Cravings might be Fulfilled without any Lusts, and without Committing any Sins — such as Fornication, Adultery, and Sodomy, which are Strictly Forbidden by all of the Gods; but, Frot Sex is not Forbidden: beCause it is Necessary for Horny Men to Relieve themselves in a Riit Waa, if they are not Married, which is the Correct and most Perfect Plan, which Means that Horny Teenagers should have Frot Sex, rather than Commit Fornication: beCause it is not Right for Teenage Girls, nor Unmarried Women to get Pregnant, which will be Understood by the Greeks, who will Teach their Boys to Wrestle Naked with one another, just to Fulfill their Natural Cravings for Flesh-to-Flesh Contact, at which Times they might Ejaculate their Sperms, which is no Sin: beCause God does not Forbid it. Therefore, do not Think of it as some Evil Thing: beCause it is much Better than Sodomy, which is Nasty, Stinking, Filthy, Demeaning, Degrading, Demoralizing, Effeminizing, and DANGEROUS, which is WHY that God Forbids it. Therefore, Abstain from it, and Learn to Hate it: beCause it is a Bad Temptation for anyone to Yield to. Moreover, when Victorious Soldiers Sodomize their Enemies, they are Committing the Worst of Immoral Acts, whereby they will have no Positions in the Kingdom of God; but, if they do not Thoroughly Repent by Means of Fasting and Praying for 40 Consecutive Days and Nights, they will be Cast Out of this Earth, into a Lower Order of Hateful Worlds, whereby they will be Tormented both Day and Night, until they Do Repent and Return to All that is Good, which is God. Therefore, God has Designed the Prostate Gland to be Extra Sensual, whereby Men might be Tested for their Goodness, just to Prove that they are Worthy of an Inheritance in the Kingdom of God, if they Pass their Tests. Therefore, be Wise, and do not Yield to the Temptations of the Devil: beCause he has nothing but Bad Rewards to Offer to his Victims, which is also True for those Ignorant People who Lust after Money and the Vain Things that it can Buy, who become Possession Worshipers, who Sell their Souls to Satan for Obtaining Possessions that no one should have to Own: beCause all of the Material Wealth of this World has been Provided Free of all Charges by the Most-High God, who Understands that everyone Needs a Good Secure House to Live in, which is Fireproof, Mouse-proof, Termite-proof, Hail-proof, Rot-proof, Paint-proof, Tornado-proof, Hurricane-proof, Flood-proof, Mudslide-proof, Avalanche-proof, Earthquake-proof, Tsunami-proof, Volcano-proof, Insurance-proof, and Tax-proof: beCause of Establishing a Righteous One-World Government, which simply Mints and Prints the Necessary New Money — not to give it away to Ignorant Fools, nor to Waste it on Needless Bankers — but, for Hiring Seven Great Armies of Working Soldiers to Help one another to Build Beautiful Planned City States, which are Designed for True Prosperity with Freedom, Liberty and Justice for all Peoples, who are Secure within their own Fortresses, which should have Hotels in the Middle of them for Visitors, which are Surrounded by many Terraced All-Mineral Organic Gardens, which Step Out and Down toward the Terraces of the Castles, which Surround the Hotels, which are Surrounded by Great Stone Terraces on the Insides and Outsides of those Castles, which Terraces are Filled with Beautiful Stone Dome Home Complexes, which Join their Luscious Gardens, which are on their Roofs, on Top of 10 to 20 feet of Dirt and Rough Rocks, which are Packed with Sand around their Ceramic-faced Water-proofed Stone Domes, which have Skylight Shafts that reach up through and well over the Dirt and Rocks and Gardens with 3 feet of Rich Topsoil, which Skylights are Covered with Heavy Steel Doors on Hinges, which can be Closed during Severe Storms and Hot or Cold Weather: beCause all such Houses must be Self-air-conditioned, having large Ice Houses for each Complex of Domes, which are Built on Top of Cisterns for Water Storage: beCause those Ice Houses can be Used Wisely for Sucking Out the Moisture within a House, in Order to keep the Humidity Low and Comfortable, in Order to Prevent Molds from Growing, which Ice can be Produced by the Electric Power that is Produced by the Wind Generators in the Stone Arcades, which Surround the Tops of all of the Tall Stone Walls of those Great Terraces around the Fortresses, which Surround the Castles, being 40 to 100 Miles in Diameter: beCause that will make it Impractical for any Army of Fools to Attack such a Beautiful Planned City State, which should also be Surrounded by 2 Large Moats full of Water, having Slick Polished Granite Inner Walls, having the Outermost Moat about 200 feet Deep and 200 feet Wide, and full of Sea Water for Sharks, Squids, Octopuses, Jellyfishes, Corals, Sea Fishes of Various Kinds, Poisonous Snakes, and other Mean Creatures to Live in, which can be Watched by Means of Underground Tunnels with Strong Windows at the Far Ends of those Tunnels: beCause, if any Invading Army Attempts to

25

Climb Over the Outermost Stone Wall, they will Slip and Fall into the Outer Moat, and Wish to God that they had been Born in some Jungle in Africa, where it is less Dangerous. However, the Innermost Moat should be full of Fresh-water Fishes and Clean Fishes, only: beCause they can be Fed and Gathered in Nets for People to Eat in Moderation, when they are Hungry for Proteins. Otherwise, they can be Gathered and Sold to whomever Lives on the Outsides of those GLORIOUS Swanky Hotels, Castles and Fortresses, who have not yet made up their Minds concerning whatever is Riit nor WRong: beCause they Suffer with Chronic Constipation of their Minds. Indeed, they have many Good Lessons to Learn, which they could easily Learn by Reading Good Books; but, they Choose to Do everything in a Difficult Way, like an Independent Jackass, who Refuses to Work with other Jackasses to Build all such Beautiful Planned City States, who makes a Fool of himself, who becomes an Education Slave, Work Slave, Tax Slave, Insurance Slave, Rent Slave, Loan Slave, Usury Slave, Home-owner Slave, ElecTrickery Bills Slave, Food Bills Slave, Water Bills Slave, Gas Bills Slave, Mortgage Bills Slave, Telephone Bills Slave, Internet Bills Slave, Entertainment Bills Slave, Drug Bills Slave, Doctor Bills Slave, Hospital Bills Slave, Transportation Bills Slave, Repair Bills Slave, Childcare Bills Slave, Credit Card Debt Bills Slave, Nursing Home Bills Slave, Funeral Home Bills Slave, and Various other Kinds of SLAVES: beCause of being Greatly Deceived by CAPITALISM, which is the Love of Money in Action, even as it shall be during the Last Days, just before the Second Coming of the Anointed Savior, when the Deceived People of the Whole Earth will be Greatly Corrupted by Capitalist Lies: beCause of Seeking the False Riches, which will not Satisfy their Souls, nor Save them from their Endless Woes. And thus, it will be: beCAUSE of the Rejection of Provable Truths, whereby it will all End with a Great ATOMIC NIGHTMARE in the Divided States of United Lies: beCause of making Enemies of GOD, who will give Satan Permission to Destroy them by FIRE: beCause they Love Abominations, and Seek after Vain Things that no one Needs for Living a Healthy nor Happy Life, even within Beautiful Swanky PALACES, which can be made in many Ways, whereby no 2 Palaces are just Alike: beCause, it only Requires a little Imagination to Do that, which most Young People have, if they Use it. Moreover, Yohoovu God Invites them to Do it: beCause he Seeks their True Prosperity; but, only IF they Learn, Believe, Love and OBEY his 20 Commandments, which are not Difficult to Learn, Believe, Love, nor Obey: beCause they are rather Simple. Therefore, Strain yourselves to Learn them, O FOOLS, before your Eyeballs Melt Out of their Sockets, and your Tongues Fall Out of your Mouths: beCause of Rejecting Provable Truths without any Justifiable Causes! Yes, you must

DEMAND a Great Worldwide TELEVISED Court HEARING, whereby you can all Learn what is GOOD for you, and what has been BAD for you, whereby you can Rightly Choose whatever you Believe is Good for you, and Live with other People of Like-mindedness, in Perfect PEACE, who all Agree to Learn, Believe, Love and OBEY those 20 Magnified Commandments, just to have TRUE Prosperity, without any Hateful Taxes! However, if anyone Objects to that Plan, they may Choose to Live in the Wilderness with Lions, Bears, Snakes, Scorpions, Spiders, Ticks, Chiggers, Fleas, Cockroaches, Bedbugs, and other Uncivilized Creatures, or whatever Mean Creatures might be Out there, who will be Multiplying, if they are left alone, who will forever be a Great THREAT to any Rebellious Children, who might be Cast Out of those GLORIOUS Swanky Hotels, Castles and Fortresses, if they do not Quickly REPENT and Change their Ways of Thinking and Living. After all, no one is Asking them to Say nor Do any Evil Things; but, only to Say and Do GOOD Things. Indeed, if they Object to having Frot Sex with the other Horny Boys, they can Masturbate themselves, and get a Whore's Forehead for Doing it, and God will not Object; but, they will only be Depriving themselves of Great Pleasures, which they could Richly Enjoy with True Love, while Practicing FIDELITY, which is the Chief Virtue with God: beCause Marriage is Honorable in all Cases, including Gay Marriages, whereby their Beds are Undefiled: beCause of Practicing FIDELITY, which is Sexual Faithfulness to just one other Person, to whom you are Married, which is a GOOD Thing; but, God will Judge and Condemn all Liars, Whoremongers, Fornicators, Adulterers, Sodomites, and whomever Disobeys his Divine LAWS: beCause no such People can Enter into his Holy Kingdom, lest they should Defile it. Therefore, make up your Minds concerning whom you will Love and Obey: beCause Satan Seeks to Obtain your Soul by any and all Means Available. Yes, it is a Fine Line to Follow along the Narrow Trail that Leads UP and OVER the Tall Mountain of the Nolij of All that is Good and Evil; but, if you make it over there, into that Beautiful Valley of Peace in the Blest Land of Perfect Oneness, in the Paradise of True Happiness on the other Side of the Jordan River, in the Promised Land, you will be very Glad that you Learned, Believed, Loved, and Obeyed those 20 Magnified Commandments, which can be Found in: **"LIGHTNING STRIKES Versus Lightning Bugs!" (HOW you can Become Moderately RICH, without Telling any Lies nor Selling any Trash!) By The Worldwide People's Revolution!® Book 074.** *Yes, it is an Amazing Book, which everyone should Carefully Study with an Open and Honest Mind. — NMV.*

02-06 [_] Well, my Friend, if any Person Reads or Hears those Inspired Words of Provable Truths, and Rejects them, on Account of some Sorry Excuse, I would say that they Deserve to be Deceived by Satan, and also get FRIED ALIVE by the Great ATOMIC NIGHTMARE: beCause of being Extremely STUPID! After all, Words hardly get any Better than *those,* which should be red Aloud on Loudspeakers from all of the Housetops of Believers, Worldwide — except that it would be Illegal in most Places, where they would call it "Communist Propaganda." However, no Communists, Socialists, Fascists, nor Capitalists ever Proposed making everyone in the World Moderately Rich in a Riit Waa: beCause that would not be in the Interests of Rich HOGS, who Want the Whole Economic Pie for themselves: beCause they have a Greedy Selfish Nature. †§‡

02-07 [_] O Great White Bald Eagle, I must Confess that you have a World View that is like none other, which I Like: beCause I Hate that Edomite Slavery System. For Example, I could Dig Up all of those Irish Potatoes within 4 Hours, and Wash them within another 4 Hours, and Store them in my Root Cellar for a Year's Supply. Therefore, why should I have to make myself into an Eternal Slave, just to Eat and Wear some Rags? Therefore, I Agree with you — that everyone Needs to be SET UP PROPERLY for Living, at HOME, whereby they can be FREE, Healthy and Happy; and not be Worried about any Hateful Viirusez, Flqz, Unemployment, Droughts, Famines, Wars, Terrorist Attacks, Rapes, Murders, Thefts, Robberies, Suicides, Sexual Harassments, Fires,

Tornadoes, Hurricanes, Earthquakes, Tsunamis, Mudslides, Landslides, nor any such Evil Things!

02-08 [_] Well, my Friend, that is what I have been Saying for more than 40 Years; but, it seems that most People are Spiritually DEAF, and cannot Hear any Provable Truths! Indeed, all of those Potatoes came from just one Row in the Garden, on less than 1-hundredth of an Acre. Therefore, if each Family had one-acre Gardens, they could easily Feed themselves with a Week or 2 of Work, if they were Tawt HOW to Do it, Properly. Therefore, why should they make Eternal Slaves of themselves, just to Eat and Wear some Rags, as you say? Indeed, they would also Need some Fruit Trees, Grape Vines, Berry Bushes, and Nut Trees, just to have a Healthy Diet.

02-09 [_] O Great White Bald Eagle, I just LOVE those Sweet Fragrant Juicy Mangos, which can be Peeled, Pitted, and Frozen in Glass Freezer Boxes with Tight Lids, which can be Stored for 5 to 10 Years, and still be GOOD, which can be Ground Up for making 100% Mango Iced-cream, without any Sugar, Cream, Spices, nor anything else: beCause they are DELICIOUS, just as they are; but, only IF they were Delicious before they were Frozen, which they would be, if they were Tree-ripened, and Harvested at the Peak of their Perfection, even as it should be for everyone! ‡

02-10 [_] Well, my Friend, that Requires **"The Swanky Associations of Working Soldiers!" (A Fascinating Collection of Various Kinds of**

Voluntary Working Soldiers!) By The Worldwide People's Revolution!® Book 018B, just to get it all Done Correctly, one of which would be "The Swanky Association of Professional All-Mineral Organic Gardeners," who would Attend to all of those Fruit Trees, Grape Vines, Berry Bushes, Nut Trees, Vegetable Gardens, Flower Gardens, and Terraced Community Gardens, which would Feed the Hordes of People, who would be coming to Visit those **"Royal Swanky Buffets!" (The Best Feasts in the Whole World!) By The Worldwide People's Revolution!®** Book 103.

— Chapter 03 —

The World's First Swanky Truth-brary!

03-01 [_] A Swanky TRUTH-brary is the Opposite of a Public LIE-brary, which is usually speld L-I-B-R-A-R-Y, which is a Collection of mostly LIES, while a Swanky Truth-brary is a Great Collection of mostly Provable Truths, and only enough Lies to Spice it all up and make it Enticing to read, being much like the *Holy Bible,* which has just enough Lies in it to Keep everyone's Attention, you might say, beginning with that Fake Adam and Eve Story, which is quickly followed by the Fake Noah's Ark Story. The Reason that I call it a Fake Adam and Eve Story, is beCause Adam and Eve had only 3 BOYS, and NO Girls, according to *Genesis;* and yet Cain went to the Land of Nod, and got himself a Wife in Chapter 4, which tells us that much of the Story is MISSING: beCause it is Obviously a Mutilated Book, whose Editors Removed almost all of the Important Details for making any Sense of it. However, it has been Revealed to the Colorful Peacock from Angel Ridge, King's Mountain, Kentucky 40442 U.S.A., that Adam and Eve had more than 100 Children, and most of them before Cain and Abel were Born. Moreover, the Earth was Populated with Millions of Black and Brown Peoples at the Time that Jehovah God Created Adam from the Elements of the Dust of the Earth, inside of the Hollow Earth, which is the Paradise of God, from which Adam and Eve were Cast Out: beCause the Tree of Life did not Die, and the Garden of Eden is still being Attended to, which is Inside of the Holy City called MOUNT ZION, which is the Holy City of the Great King, who is Jesus Christ, himself, who now Governs it, who went to Prepare a Place for his Saints to Escape from the Great Tribulation; but, only IF they Believe the Provable Truths that have been Revealed to his Selected King, who has Come to get the Household of Israel in Order:

beCause Jesus Christ is not going to Marry an Unholy Bride, or Unclean Church. ‡

03-02 [_] So, it is very Important that all such Good News is Tawt to everyone in the World, as much as that is Possible, which is the Basic Reason for Building Swanky Truth-braries all around the World, which are Special Book Stores, which contain all of the Available Books of the Colorful Peacock from Angel Ridge, most of which have been Lost — Thanks to Bill Computer Software Gates and his Updating Nonsense, which made the Original Books Obsolete: beCause that Software does not Translate Correctly into the Updated Software in Modern Computers. At least I cannot make it Work, which is Okay: beCause most People will find it Difficult to read only 100 Books, without reading 365 Books. However, it is a very Sad Story: beCause many of those Original Books were of Higher Qualities than most of the later Books, which the Colorful Peacock had spent Months UPDATING, only to be Destroyed by some Mormons, who had a Failing Computer System, or Server. Whatever the Case, the Holy Spirit did not Die; and the Words can be Revealed again, if God Wants us to have them. In Fact, even Better Words could be Revealed, if God Wanted us to have them. It all goes the Way that it does to Teach us to not Trust anyone. Hundreds of Books and thousands of Pictures were Lost, which should have been Saved on DVDs or CDs. All such Books should have been Saved in Book Forms, in Real Print; but, Extreme Poverty was not Able to Do that. So, it is Hoped that Swanky Truth-braries will make it Possible to Save the Books in Print.

03-03 [_] The Truth-braries should be Secure Fireproof Stone Domes, much like the Pantheon in Rome, having very THICK Solid Stone Walls, and Solid Concrete Roofs, which should be 60 feet Wide on the Inside Diameters, whereby a Book Display can be Set Up in the Centers of those Large Domes, which Book Display is 8 feet High and Wide and 12 feet Long, having 2 Doorways at the Ends, much like this Top View Shows:

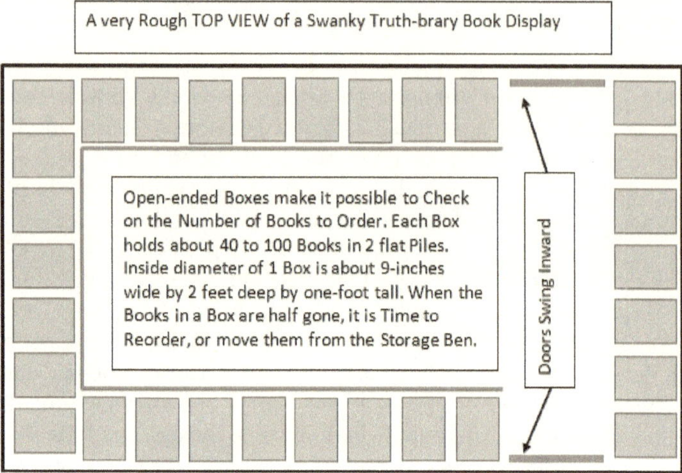

There are Rows of little Glass Doors (about 1 foot tall and 9 inches wide) with Books behind the Glass, facing outward, all around the Book Display. The Reader simply Opens a little Door, and gets out the Book that he Wants to Read or Buy.

03-04 [_] Books that are not Selling very Well should be placed in the Boxes on the far Corners of the Book Display, on the left end: beCause those Boxes cannot be seen from Inside the Book Display. The Books in the Corner Boxes must be placed in the Boxes from Outside, by Opening each little Glass Door, which is actually a Special Picture Frame on Hinges, with a Book behind the Glass within the Frame, facing outward, which Book is not Removed, unless the Cover looks Faded, which might require several Years to do that Fading. The Back Cover of the Book should also be behind Glass on the Backside of the Picture Frame, which can be read when the little Door is Opened. The Lowest Box should be at least 2 feet above the Floor Level: so that no one must Bend Over very much to get a Book, nor to Replace some Books that have been Sold. Likewise, the Boxes should not be too High for People to easily Reach into them. They should be a Maximum of 4 feet High; or, a Maximum of 6 feet at the Top from the Floor. In other words, 8 Horizontal Rows and 4 Vertical Rows on the 2 Sides of the Book Display, and 7 Horizontal Rows 4 High on the Ends of the Book Display, for a Total of 120 Book Display Boxes.

03-05 [_] Here is an Example of what one Book Display Box might look like, if your Imagination can make it out Correctly. It is a Front View, looking straight at the Box Picture Frame, which is a little too Wide and

Tall to be Realistic in its Dimensions; but, it does give to you a Good Idea concerning what it should Look like, in general. It is actually pretty Good for the Word for Windows Drawing Program.

The Picture Frame must be made of Tough Varnished Wood, which can easily carry the Weight of the 2 Sheets of ¼-inch-thick Glass, plus the Weight of the Book and the Frame on small Strong 2-inch-high Hinges.

The Latch on the Door must be Stainless Steel and Secure.

03-06 [_] Now, just Fit any Book that is 8.5-inches by 11-inches into the Picture Frame, which is Mounted on the Wooden Box that is behind it. Otherwise, those Boxes should have Facing Boards on the Front Edges, which are Fastened to the Boxes Securely; and the Picture Frames are Mounted onto the Facing Boards, which Looks much Nicer, even though it will Raise the Height of the entire Display by a couple of Inches, which is Okay, which is no Problem: because, if anyone is too Short to Reach a Higher Box, they can Ask for some Help, or get on Top of an 8-inch-high Stepping Stool, which can be left in front of the Book Display for People to Trip over and Wake them Up. §

03-07 [_] The next Drawings show a TOP VIEW of the entire Dome Complex with Entrance, Storage Bens, Café, Rest Rooms, and so on. This Plan is to make a Self-air-conditioned Truth-brary with at least 40 Comfortable Recliners or Swanky Easy Chairs for Visitors and Readers to Sit in, who may go to Sleep, and when they Wake Up again, they can continue to Read. They should not be Disturbed, unless they are Homeless People, who Need to take Showers and Wash their Clothes, who should be Welcome to Do that in the Appropriate Rooms, which are a Part of the Complex. They should not be Invited to Eat, until they have taken a Shower and put on Clean Robes, nor until they have red at least a few Pages of a given Book, and can Pass a Test concerning whatever they red: beCause that is the Price that they must Pay for something to Eat, which is not a Bad Idea. Much of the Foods will come from the Organic Garden on the Roof of the Complex, which will be Good Foods, if they are Hungry enough. Otherwise, the Foods might be Imported from other Swanky Organic Gardens. After all, the Main Function of a Swanky Truth-brary is to EDUCATE People in All Ways, both Physically, Mentally, and Spiritually.

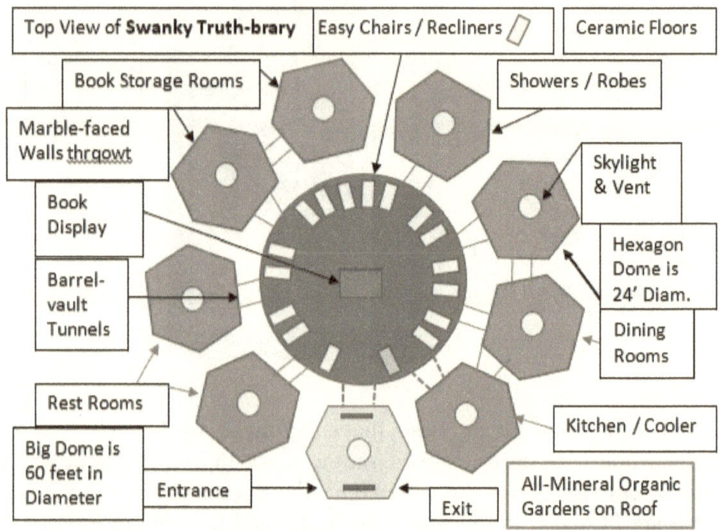

03-08 [_] So, all of the Walls must be Covered with Polished Marble Tiles, except in the Kitchens, Dining Rooms, Rest Rooms, and Bathroom Domes, which can be Hexagons, Octagons, or even Dodecagons. The Large Central Domes can also be Dodecagons, whereby they have Flat Walls to Set Marble Tiles on, which makes a much Nicer Dome, than if it were merely Painted: beCause the Marble is Inspiring. Each Section of a Dodecagon could have a Different Kind of Marble on it, just to Show the many Great Varieties of Marbles that are Available in this World of Wonders; but, I Prefer to have only 2 Kinds, with a Pattern of Light and Dark Marbles on every other Section of the Wall in the large Dome. Other Kinds of Marble can be put in the Entrance, Dining Domes, and Book Storage Domes; but, few People will get to See the Storage Domes. Therefore, some "Ugly" Marbles can be put on the Walls of those Domes. Rest Rooms can also have Marble.

03-09 [_] O Great White Bald Eagle, will the Recliners lie down FLAT, whereby the Readers can Sleep? Will they come with Pillows, also?

03-10 [_] Well, my Friend, those Recliners will be made as Comfortable as Possible: so that Readers can Sleep Soundly, if they Want to, and also with Pillows: beCause there are not very many People left Alive, who Like to Read Books very much. In Fact, most of the People will be coming just to get a Shower, a Clean Robe, and to Eat and Sleep, while Pretending to Read Books. However, other People will come to Buy Books, and take them Home to Read, or Give them to Poor Strangers, Friends, Naaberz, or Relatives. It is only Hoped that after X-amount of Time, the Masses of People will Learn a few Things, and even take up Fasting and Praying as a Spiritual Exercise; but no one should Count on it, until someone becomes like Moses or Elijah.

— Chapter 04 —

How are the Children supposed to Save themselves from the Great ATOMIC NIGHTMARE?

04-01 [_] This is the Saddest Part of this Tale of Warning: beCause the Children are Trapped in Cities of Confusion, with no Way to Escape, unless their Parents Move OUT with them, which some will no doubt Do; but, most will not: beCause they have a Doomsday Attitude, and even Hope to Die during the Atomic Nightmare: beCause they cannot Visualize a Better Life within **"Beautiful Swanky PALACES!" (A New Concept in Living Habits — Swanky Palaces for Poor People!) By The Worldwide People's Revolution!®** Book 066. In Fact, they Visualize themselves Working in HOT Fields, bending over all Day Long to Harvest Tomatoes, Cucumbers, Bell Peppers, Green Leaves, Green Onions, Heavy Watermelons, Cantaloupes, Potatoes, or whatever: beCause they do not have the Faith to Study the Wonderful Inspired Books of the Colorful Peacock from Angel Ridge, who Proposes that everyone does a Moderate Amount of Work in their own Private Gardens — such as 15 to 20 Minutes of Work per Workday, on Average: beCause it can easily be Proven that 15 to 20 Minutes of Work per Workday will keep a Family Well-fed, if the Gardener Knows What to Do, When to Do it, and How to Do it. Most People have no Idea: beCause it is something that is not Tawt in any Public Schools of Ignorant Fools, whose Goal is to make as many People into Slaves as Possible, which they are Presently Succeeding at. In Fact, they are the People who Discourage Children from even Reading Inspired Books, whereby 80% of High School Graduates never read another Book during the Remaining Years of their Lives! So, that is a Real Success Story, you might say, for Greedy Selfish Slave Masters and Capitalists, whereby tens of thousands of the Slaves Commit Suicide, each Year: beCause of having a Bleak Hopeless Future to Look Forward to as Drug Addicts.

www.who.int › prevention › suicide › suicideprevent ▾
Suicide data - WHO
Close to 800 000 **people** die due to **suicide every year**, which is one person **every** 40 ... sub-population **and** individual levels to prevent **suicide and suicide attempts**. There are indications that **for each** adult who died by **suicide** there **may** have ...

An estimated quarter million **people each year** become **suicide** survivors (AAS). There is one **suicide for every** estimated 25 **suicide attempts**. (CDC). There is ...

AFSP's latest data on **suicide** are taken from the Centers **for** Disease Control **and** ... **year for** which data are available), approximately 575,000 **people** visited **a** hospital **for** ... Adult females reported **a suicide attempt** 1.4 times as often as males.

04-02 [_] So, O Great White Bald Eagle, what are the Innocent Children supposed to DO to Save themselves? What are Poor Helpless People supposed to Do, since they cannot Afford to MOVE OUT of their Cities of Confusion; and would not even know where to Go to, to Survive? ‡

04-03 [_] Well, my Friend, it is for Certain that I cannot go from Door to Door, nor from City to City, in Order to WARN all of them, and maybe Waste an entire Day, just Attempting to Convert or Change the Mind of a single Person. So, they will just have to DIE! What else can they Do? †§‡

04-04 [_] O Great White Bald Eagle, they Need some HAWKS and Screech Owls to Scream at them! They need another Billy Sunday, or Billy Graham to Preach to them. They need some Hellfire and Brimstone Sermons!

04-05 [_] Well, my Friend, they seem to be a Lost Generation, and the Ministers are only in Business for Gaining more Money, who have no Real Interest in anyone's Salvation. Therefore, it will Require some Mighty Miracles, just to get their Attention; and then, someone will have to Dig the Wax of Unbelief Out of their Inner Spiritual Ears, whereby they might Understand a few **"IMPORTANT THINGS that Should Have Been Written in the Holy Bible!" (A Special Challenge to all Professing Christians, Jews, Hindus, Muslims and Atheists!) By The Irreverent Penname Scumbag!** § Book 110.

04-06 [_] O Great White Bald Eagle, what this World most Desperately Needs is a TYRANT KING, who Forces the People to Say and Do whatever is Proven to be Good for them, whereby all of the Innocent Children can be Saved Alive, if they are Healthy enough to Survive. Most of them are being Fed Junk Foods and Poisonous Drinks, whereby it is Amazing that any of them are still Alive. God Knows that they are the Most Vulnerable Victims of Capitalism. Therefore, I Suggest that you get up on a Soap Box in Hyde Park, in London, England, and Proclaim yourself to be that TYRANT KING, whereby you can Challenge anyone to Prove your **"Guaranteed Solutions!" (HOW to Solve our Local and Global Problems in the Most-Rational Manner Possible!)** Book 080, to be WRong or Unworkable, just to Discover whether or not you get any Response from them. Otherwise, you could put your Book Display on a Trailer, and Drag it around.

04-07 [_] Trust me, just one Look at me in my White Robe with the Blue Trim, and they would all Walk Away.

Why is Westminster Abbey famous?

The current **Westminster Abbey** was started by Henry III in 1245 and is "one of the most important Gothic buildings in the country, with the medieval shrine of an Anglo-Saxon saint still at its heart." ... **Westminster Abbey** has been the coronation church for the British Monarch since 1066. Jul 17, 2015

www.guidelondon.org.uk › blog › major-london-sites › 1...
11 Facts About Westminster Abbey | Guide London

04-08 [_] O Great White Bald Eagle, I say that you Need the POWER of GOD, whereby you can Transform Rough Rocks into PURE GOLD, which will get their Attention, and Keep it for at least 10 Minutes, which will give to you enough Time to Raise Up Abraham Lincoln from the Dead, which will Hold their Attention for another 20 Minutes or so, which will give to you enough Time to Raise Up some Woolly Mammoth Elephants for them to Gaze at, which will Keep their Attention for a Day or 2, which will give to you enough Time to Ride one of those Elephants to Rochester, New York, where the Deaf Children go to, whom you can Heal, all at once; which will get their Attention, until you can Visit the Used and Abused Veterans of those Hateful Wars, whom you can also Heal and Restore their Lost Limbs and Organs, which will get their Attention for a Month or 2, which will give to you enough Time to Ride on that Elephant to London, to Visit the Queen of England, who, in the Meantime, can Invite the Pope of Rome and the European Leaders to Westminster Abbey for a Conference with you, whereby you can give to them your Famous *Declaration of Interdependence* Speech, which can be found in an Inspired Book, called: **"The Low Court of Supreme Injustices is Brought to Trial!"** **(Our Selected King Butts Heads with the United States Supreme Court, with or without their Black Robes of Hypocrisies and Lies!) By The Worldwide People's Revolution!®** Book 011, which is a Companion Book of **"The Right Design for Living!" (A List of 5,000 Advantages for Building Beautiful Planned City States!) By The Worldwide People's Revolution!®** Book 012C. Yes, after that Beautiful Speech, you can Read Aloud: **"Our Selected King SPEAKS OUT!"** (**It is High Time for some Sane Person to get Total Control of this Insane World!) By The Worldwide People's Revolution!®** Book 100, which is a Companion Book of: **"The Gospel According to our Elected King!" (The Good News from the Most-Modern Perspective!) By The Worldwide People's Revolution!®** Book 077, which Contains the Famous Sermon of JONAH to the People of Nineveh, whereby 120,000 or more People were Converted to the Truth during just ONE DAY! Yes, the Queen will Invite you to Read that Inspired Book Aloud in her Palace to all Ears that can Hear, whereby 7 Billion People will be Converted to the Truth during just ONE DAY! †§‡§§

04-09 [_] Well, my Friend, I Think that you are getting your Hopes a little too High at this Time: beCause, it is very Unlikely that George Warmonger Bush and Little Dick Chicanery will Accept all such Provable Truths, much less, the Fake Trumpeter and his Puppet Staff in the Little White Outhouse, in George Washington's Backyard, which Stinks to the Highest Heaven with Ancient Political Republican Lies and Fresh Political Democratic Donkey Dung, which the Trumpeter has been Farting Out of his Mouth, while his Followers have been Sucking it Up, who should all be Fasting and Praying, according to: **"The Proper RULES for FASTING!" (The Complete Instruction Manual for True Repentance!) By The Worldwide People's Revolution!®** Book 046, which is a Companion Book of: **"HOW to Become a HOLY Man!" (40 Good Reasons WHY People Should FAST and PRAY!) By The Worldwide People's Revolution!®** Book 045: beCause, when a Person gets Sick or Badly Wounded, he just Naturally Loses his Appetite, which is a Warning Sign to STOP EATING, which, if he Cheerfully OBEYS, he will get Well again: beCause that is HOW the Body Cleanses itself from Unwanted Poisons and Stinking Filth, which Feeds the Germs and Worms, which must be EXPELLED FROM THE BODY, in Order to Save it Alive, which is WHY Sick People Vomit and get Diarrheas, whereby Gallons of Poisons are EXPELLED, which Saves their Lives! Otherwise, they would DIE from those Toxic Poisons! Therefore, Educate yourself about that Subject: beCause the Doctor

Knife, Doctor Pill Popper, Doctor Pus Shots, and Doctor Insanity are only in Business for the MONEY — not for your Good Health, which is WHY that Jesus did not Send anyone to them for Help: beCause he Understood that every Body was Created in such a Way as to Heal ITSELF, without the Assistance of any SNAKES with their Poisons. Indeed, Moses also Understood the same Thing, and told the Lepers to go Outside of the Camp and Fast for 10 Days, in *Leviticus 13 and 14,* and then Return to be Inspected by the Priests, and then Fast for another Week, just to make Sure that they were Cured from it, which Worked quite Well for about 1,500 Years, until the Time of Jesus, when he Perceived that they Needed to Suffer for another 2,000 Years, or more, just to come to their Right Senses with *the Prodigal Son of Luke 15.* So, that is where most People are Stuck in the Mud, and cannot Drag themselves Out: beCause of being Bogged Down with Endless Bills to Pay, whereby they are all SLAVES of Various Kinds and Colors, whom you might Imagine would be Ready to Listen to the Man with the Spirit of Elijah; but, they are NOT: beCause they have been Greatly DECEIVED, whereby they do not Realize it: beCause, how can a Deceived Person Realize that he is Deceived? Indeed, his Mind would have to be Enlightened by the Inspired Words of Provable Truths, which he would have to STUDY with a Humble Honest Open Mind! But, behold, how can a Deceived Person DO that, seeing that he Sincerely Believes a HUGE Pack of Outlandish Capitalist LIES? Yes, he Believes in the False OWNERSHIP Doctrine, whereby he Believes that he must get enough Money for Buying an almost Worthless Wooden / Plastic Firetrap Mouse-infested Cockroach Den, whereby he can make an Eternal Interest Slave and Tax Slave of himself, just to Pay for it, 3 or 4 Times; and therefore, in Order to Obtain that Money, he must make an Education Slave of himself, just to get that Deplorable Diploma, whereby he can get a so-called "Good Job," at just a little more than Minimum Wages, whereby he becomes a Credit Card Debt Slave: beCause he never has enough Money to get himself Set Up Properly for Living. In Fact, he must make himself into a Transportation Slave, just to get himself to that Boring Capitalist Job, and take a Chance on getting Killed in his New Car, which Belongs to the Bank; but, he calls it HIS CAR, as if he Owned it: beCause he likes to LIE to himself, which his Friends and Naaberz also do: beCause none of them are Perfectly HONEST about anything: beCause they cannot Afford to BE Perfectly Honest, lest they should have to REPENT and Change their Ways of Thinking and Living, which is Far too PAINFUL for a PROUD Owner of a Wooden / Plastic Firetrap Mouse-infested Cockroach Den and some Old Rusty Gas-hog Vehicle, which Requires him to make an Insurance Slave of himself, just to Drive it, Legally, lest he should be Fined for being a "Bad Boy," who does not Play by the Capitalist RULES, which Require that all of the Work Slaves must also be Tax Slaves, Insurance Slaves, Rent Slaves, Home-owner Slaves, Interest Slaves, Mortgage Slaves, Telephone Bills Slaves, ElecTrickery Bills Slaves, Food Bills Slaves, Water Bills Slaves, Gas Bills Slaves, Transportation Bills Slaves, Repair Bills Slaves, Drug Bills Slaves, Doctor Bills Slaves, Hospital Bills Slaves, Childcare Bills Slaves, Nursing Home Bills Slaves, and Funeral Home Bills Slaves: beCause that is HOW those Lying Conniving Edomites have Arranged it for their Ignorant Spiritually-Blind PROUD SLAVES, who are too Proud to Confess it! But, I will Confess it for them: beCause I am a Humble Honest Person, and perhaps the First such Person that those Slaves ever Heard of, whose Spiritual Eyes are Covered with Capitalist GREASE, Butter and Honey! †§‡

04-10 [_] O Great White Bald Eagle, I must Confess that I never did Think of myself as a SLAVE, until Today, after you Enlightened my Mind about it all. Moreover, I Attempted to Explain it to my Son; but, he was too Busy Playing his Video Games, and could not Hear anything that I was Saying. Therefore, HOW am I supposed to Save his Soul from a Lifetime of Self-inflicted Torments as a General All-American SLAVE of the Most-Ignorant Kind?

— Chapter 05 —

HOW the Slaves can be LIBERATED!

05-01 |_| First of all, the Readers must Do their Small Parts to Educate their Friends, Relatives and Naaberz, by Sharing Copies of this Inspired Book with them, whereby they might Educate themselves by Reading the Book. Secondly, after this Book has been Spread Out, Far and Wide, the Masses of People will be DEMANDING: **"The GREAT Worldwide TELEVISED Court HEARING!" (That Great Meeting of the Most-Intelligent and Well-Educated Minds!) By The Worldwide People's Revolution!®** Book 041B, whereby we will SHUT OFF all Nonsense on TV Channels, and Use those Televisions WISELY, in Order to Enlighten the Minds of everyone in the Whole World, whereby the Masses of People will DEMAND that we Establish: **"The New RIGHTEOUS One-World Government!" (HOW to Establish a Righteous One-World Government without Going to WAR!) By The Worldwide People's Revolution!®** Book 056, which is a Companion Book of: **"101 Good Reasons and Great Advantages for Establishing a Righteous One-World Government!" (Government By the People, Of the People, and For the People!) By The Worldwide People's Revolution!®** Book 104. In other Words, it will be **"The END of CONFUSION!" (The Magnificent Wedding of the Most-Humble Honest Nations, and the Grand Year of JUBILEE!) By The Worldwide People's Revolution!®** Book 050: beCause the Masses of People will Gladly Choose to Live within those **"Beautiful Swanky PALACES!" (A New Concept in Living Habits — Swanky Palaces for Poor People!) By The Worldwide People's Revolution!®** Book 066: beCause of being Sick of their Extreme Poverty and Endless Bills to Pay. Indeed, they will Discover that as little as 2 to 4 Hours of Common Skilled Labor per Workday is Sufficient for them to Live like Kingz and Kweenz: beCause of Wisely Using Mechanical Slaves for doing most of the Difficult Work. Therefore, they will Liberate themselves from all Slavery by simply OBEYING their Elected KING, who will Call for **"Seven Great Armies of Working Soldiers!" (HOW to Provide a Way for Everyone to WORK: so as to Eliminate Poverty, Crimes, Drug Abuses, Prisons and Unnecessary Taxes!) By The Worldwide People's Revolution!®** Book 015B, who might have to be DRAFTED Working Soldiers, if they do not Cheerfully Join one or the other of the first 6 Kinds, whereby the Seventh Army of Working Soldiers will be Paid half as much, and get Worked twice as long: beCause of being like Stubborn Spoiled Mules, who can Work on Underground Railroads, Tunnels, and Cisterns: beCause of not being Trusted to Do Good Work, as a Voluntary Working Soldier might Do, who is just Naturally more Cooperative, who can be Tawt HOW to Work Correctly: beCause of being Meek and Teachable. Indeed, they will all be HIRED to Build those **"GLORIOUS Swanky Hotels Castles and Fortresses!" (Beautiful Planned City States for WISE Intelligent and Well-Educated People with Common Sense and Good Understanding!) By The Worldwide People's Revolution!®** Book 019B: beCause everyone in the Whole World NEEDS the SECURITY of a Swanky Fortress, which is Designed for Good Self-Defense, whereby Military Weapons will become Obsolete: beCause no such Strong Fortresses can be Defeated. †§‡

05-02 [_] O Great White Bald Eagle, getting your Readers to Cooperate with you will be the First Major Obstacle to Overcome: beCause, only one Person or so in 100 even Likes to Read Books; and most of them only like Sexy Romance Novels, or Murder Mysteries: beCause they Use all such Literature to Distract their Minds from the Realities of Life, which is a Means of Escapism, you might say. Therefore, Good Luck with Persuading any Boneheads to Cooperate with you. †§‡
05-03 [_] Well, my Friend, if they do NOT Cooperate with me, they will likely find themselves in the Midst of one of those Big MUSHROOM CLOUDS of Radioactive DUST, as Corpses!

A new study reveals large diesel **trucks** to be the greatest contributors to harmful black carbon emissions close to major roadways, indicating that **vehicle** types matter **more than** traffic volume for near-road air **pollution**. Exercise your consumer right to opt out. Sep 10, 2018

www.sciencedaily.com › releases › 2018/09
Large trucks are biggest culprits of near-road air pollution ...

Seventy-five percent of carbon monoxide emissions come from automobiles. In urban areas, harmful automotive emissions are responsible for anywhere between 50 and 90 percent of air **pollution**.

05-04 [_] O Great White Bald Eagle, some Ignorant People will Blame YOU for Causing it: beCause of Speaking Evil of the Goddess called "CAPITALISM," which System is the Economic Salvation of Mankind, which was in Extreme Poverty, until the Industrial Revolution got them Out of it! Indeed, we now have more Wealth by a hundred Times, than People had in 1800. Therefore, I would say that we are doing quite Well, when Compared with those Evil Days, when most People Worked for 16 Hours per Day, just to Survive: beCause they did not have FREE ElecTrickery! — much less, all of the Convenient Electrical Appliances,

Power Tools, nor Sweet-smelling Diesel Trucks, which can Account for 20% of the Pollution in this World of Woes, while Airplanes Account for 20% of the Pollution, and Factories 20%, and other Vehicles and Houses 40%. But, no matter how you Add it all up, the Chief Offender is MANKIND, who should be Extinctified by Hydrogen BOMBS being Dropped on all Major Cities of Confusion, which are Designed Perfectly for all such Bombs to get Rid of them! Yes, that is the Best Way to Liberate all of the Slaves! †§‡

The land area **of the** entire **United States** is 3,531,905 **square miles**.

statesymbolsusa.org › national-us › uncategorized › states…

U.S. States by Size in Square Miles - State Symbols USA

Highbush **blueberries** will produce a small crop, approximately 2,000 pints per acre, in the third year. Fruit production will increase until the plants are about five years old, with average **yields** of 6,000 pints per acre possible under optimum conditions. Jul 7, 2017

extension.psu.edu › highbush-blueberry-production

Highbush Blueberry Production - Penn State Extension

05-05 [_] Well, my Enemy, and Enemy of all of Mankind, that might seem to be Reasonable to YOU; but, not to anyone who is Truly Educated: beCause this World is not Overpopulated, yet; and it could Contain a hundred Times as many People, and still not be Overpopulated, if those People were Living within those **"GLORIOUS Swanky Hotels Castles and Fortresses!"**: beCause they are Designed to Feed, Water and House 10 Times as many People as any City of Confusion — none of which Feed nor Water themselves! However, the People of Japan will likely Disagree with me about that: beCause of not Realizing how much SPACE there is in China, Russia, and wherever. For Example, all of the 8 Billion People in this World of Wonders could be Fitted quite Nicely within the United States of America, if it were Managed Properly: beCause there are no less than 1,280,000,000 Acres of mostly Farmland, which can be Placed within Great Stone TERRACES, and made 10 Times as Productive as it Presently is: beCause of Vertical Farming. For Example, one Black Walnut Tree can Produce 40 Bushels of Walnuts on a single Tree that only takes up one-27th of an Acre, or 1,600 square feet of Space, which Means that one Acre could Comfortably Contain 24 Black Walnut Trees, or 40 English Walnut Trees, or 120 Hazelnut Trees, or 2,500 Blueberry Bushes, which can Produce 6,000 Pints of Blueberries. So, how many Pints can a Family Eat during a Year? Trust me, they would do Well to Eat 10 Pints per

Person: beCause of all of the other Good Things that can be Grown and Eaten.

www.wyzant.com › Resources › Ask an Expert ▾

How many trees should be planted on an acre in order to get ...

3 answers

Oct 15, 2014 - An apple farm yields an average of 30 **bushels of apples** per tree when 20 trees are planted on **an acre** of ground. Each time 1 more tree is ...

A **bushel** of **apples** typically holds about 125 medium **apples**. That's enough to make 15 (or more) quarts of applesauce or around 15 **apple** pies. If you eat one **apple** a day, a **bushel** will last you for three months. A **bushel** of peaches is defined as 50 pounds in Georgia. May 9, 2019

Figuring that a bushel of **apples** weighs about 40 **pounds**, an **acre** of trees at this density should produce at least 16,000 **pounds** of fruit, and on a good site, with favorable climatic conditions and excellent management, as **much** as 20,000 **pounds**. May 1, 2018

fruit.umn.edu › content › before-start-apple-orchard

Before you start an apple orchard | Minnesota Fruit Research

They calculated the total cost of producing certified organic **apples** under this scenario at $11,407 per **acre**, compared with a total of $10,757 in the conventional Gala study. Assuming a return of $250 a bin, the net revenue for the conventional Gala **apples** would be $1,743 per **acre**. Jan 1, 2011

www.goodfruit.com › figuring-out-profitability

Figuring out profitability | Good Fruit Grower

Apple orchards with **standard** 20 to 30 foot spacing produce between 20,000 and 30,000 **apples per acre**. Recent high yield plantings of 500 **trees per acre** in comparison double production. A 4-**acre** Crop Circle orchard can double that again to over 100,000 **apples per acre**.

treeplantation.com › fruit-trees

FRUIT TREES – crop circle orchards - TREE PLANTATION

The price range for **apples** wholesale (such as at large real farm markets and at orchards) was between $15 to $30 per bushel, depending upon the variety and location. Popular varieties, like Gala, Fuji, Honeycrisp, etc. were around $22 - $26/bushel (wholesale).

pickyourown.org › USapplecrop

U.S. Apple Crop Facts - PickYourOwn.org

The 5 Most Expensive Trees in the World

- Sandalwood-- $20,000 per tree. ...
- African Blackwood-- $10,000 per kilogram. ...
- Agar Wood-- $10,000 per kilogram. ...
- Bocote-- $30 per board. ...
- Pink Ivory-- $8 per board.

www.tarzantreevb.com › company › blog › 44-the-5-mos...
The 5 Most Expensive Trees in the World - Tarzan Tree Service

Macadamia nuts are the most expensive nuts in the world, at $25 per pound.
Mar 6, 2019

www.businessinsider.com › macadamia-nuts-most-expensi...
Why are macadamia nuts the most expensive nuts in the world ...

Walnuts - **King of Nuts**. In health benefits, walnuts rank above peanuts, almonds, pecans, pistachios and other **nuts**. Just a handful of walnuts contain antioxidants that are two to fifteen times more powerful than vitamin E, which protects the body against ageing.

alalali.com › eng › tip_popup
Walnuts - King of Nuts

Black **walnut** logs bring premium **prices**, and have since the 1700s, with single **trees** bringing up to $20,000. Bruce Thompson, author of "Black **Walnut** For Profit," estimates a **mature** stand of black **walnut trees** can bring about $100,000 per acre in timber value alone. Sep 22, 2019

www.profitableplantsdigest.com › growing-walnut-trees-f...
Growing Walnut Trees For Profit - Profitable Plants Digest

Why are mixed nuts so expensive?

Tree **nuts** are in general **expensive** to produce, and they can't be planted in most of the world, because the soils and weather are not suitable. A farmer has to invest something in the order of $50,000 per acre over the course of four to seven years before he sees a nickel of income from a nut orchard.

www.quora.com › Why-are-nuts-so-expensive-Even-whe...
Why are nuts so expensive? Even when they're grown locally, they

Most nuts appear to be generally healthy, though some may have more heart-healthy nutrients than others. For example, **walnuts** contain high amounts of omega-3 fatty acids. **Almonds**, macadamia nuts, hazelnuts and pecans also appear to be quite heart healthy.

www.mayoclinic.org › in-depth › nuts › art-20046635
Nuts and your heart: Eating nuts for heart health - Mayo Clinic

Eat them RAW for Better Health.

two to five years

Years to Production

A first hazelnut crop can be expected within **two to five years** of planting the tree. The initial crops are usually small, but as the tree matures, the crops increase in size. A mature hazelnut tree can produce up to 25 pounds of nuts in a single year. Dec 14, 2018

homeguides.sfgate.com › Garden › Gardening ▾
How Long Does It Take a Hazelnut Tree to Produce Nuts ...

05-06 [_] I asked Google: How Long does it take to Grow a Hazelnut Tree?

Yet, **hazelnut** trees are native to the eastern half North America from Louisiana to Georgia in the south, to Manitoba and Quebec in the north. The native **hazelnut** trees (Corylus americana) are hardy, disease resistant and are very tolerant of a wide range of **growing** conditions, and yet there is a shortage of nuts. Oct 3, 2016

smallfarms.cornell.edu › 2016/10 › hazelnut-trees-are-easy
Hazelnut Trees Are Easy! - Cornell Small Farms

Hazelnut price is **$0.70** per pound or **$1,400** per ton. 9. The full production yield is 2,800 marketable pounds per acre. Commercial yields begin in the third year and full production is reached in year 12.

arec.oregonstate.edu › oaeb › files › pdf › EM8748-E
The Costs and Returns of Establishing and Producing Hazelnuts in

05-07 [_] Is that WHY that I saw a one-pound Package of Hazelnuts in their Shells for $4.98, just the other Day? The Farmer should be getting $3 per Pound, the Trucker $1, and the Store $1, to be Perfectly Fair about it. But, at any Swanky Fortress, you could Eat all that you might Want for FREE: beCause your 4 Hours of Common Skilled Labor per Workday easily Covers all of the Costs of Living, which can be Proven in a Courtroom. In Fact, I would say that a Well-Organized Swanky Fortress might have as little as 2 Hours of Work per Workday, and everyone would be Living like Royalties! After all, how many Hazelnuts (Filberts) can you Eat, before you are Satisfied? I had a dozen or so Almonds with some Raisins for Lunch, and I am Perfectly Satisfied. But, of course, I am not doing very much Work, whereby just a little Food keeps me Satisfied, which would be True for most of the People at Swanky Fortresses, once they were all Finished, and Ready to Live in them. In Fact, I can stay Fat by just Drinking a few Cups of Fruit Juice per Day, or by Eating a few Teaspoons of Honey; but, I am not a

Powerhouse of Energy by any Means: beCause, writing Books does not Require very much Energy. I have a Comfortable Easy Chair. ‡

So **1** ton of **grapes** yields about 60 cases, or 720 bottles. **A** low-yielding **1-acre** vineyard that yields 2 tons of **grapes** makes about 120 cases, or 1,440 bottles, while **an acre** that yields 10 tons produces about 600 cases, or 7,200 bottles. Jul 27, 2016

www.winespectator.com › articles › how-many-bottles-... ▾
How many bottles of wine can be made from a 1-hectare ...

The largest bunch of **grapes** is 10.12 kg (22.31 lbs) and was achieved by Sebastián Gómez Falcón and Delegación de Agricultura del Ayuntamiento de Los Palacios y Villafranca (both Spain) in Los Palacios y Villafranca, Spain, as verified on 4 August 2018. Aug 4, 2018

www.guinnessworldrecords.com › world-records › larg... ▾
Largest bunch of grapes | Guinness World Records

The estimated total **world production** for **grapes** in 2017 was 74,276,583 metric tonnes, down 1.0% from 74,992,047 tonnes in 2016. China was the **largest producer of grapes**, accounting for 16.8% of global **production**. Italy came second at 10.9%, followed by the United States at 9.6%.

Italy remains the world's largest wine producer, followed by France and Spain. These countries are also the world's largest exporters, accounting for more than 50% of the global market by volume. Apr 15, 2019

www.beveragedaily.com › Article › 2019/04/15 › Global-...
Global wine production reaches record level - Beverage Daily

Top Apple Producing Countries In The World

Rank	Country	Apples Produced (Tonnes)
1	China	44,447,793
2	United States	4,649,323
3	Poland	3,604,271
4	Turkey	2,925,828

Who has the best wine in the world?

Italy emerged victorious due to the abundance of **wine** tasting experiences on offer throughout its 21 **wine** regions running from the **top** to the bottom of its boot. France came second, Spain third and South Africa fourth, while Australia was considerably down the list in 15th place and the US way down at number 27. Jul 17, 2019

www.thedrinksbusiness.com › 2019/07 › italy-named-wor...
Italy named the world's best wine country - The Drinks Business

Which Country Drinks the Most Wine?

| 2 | Vatican City | 56.2 |

05-08 [_] That is 56.2 Liters per Capita, per Year, or a little over one Liter per Week.

What is the biggest grape in the world?

A number of different grapes have laid claim to being the world's largest at one time or another but only Japan's **Ruby Roman** grapes are both huge in size as well as in price. In 2009, a Japanese hotel manager paid a whopping $910 for a 1.5 pound (700g) bunch of tomato-red Ruby Romans. Jan 31, 2012

www.momtastic.com › webecoist › 2012/01/31 › berry-b...
Berry Berry Big: The World's 10 Largest Fruits - WebEcoist -
Which color grapes are healthiest?

There are several **colors** of **grapes**, including red, black, purple or blue (Concord), green (which is used to make white wine), pink and yellow. "Although all types of **grapes** are healthy, red **grapes** and Concord **grapes** are higher in flavonoids and phytonutrients, including resveratrol," said Rumsey. Apr 28, 2016

www.livescience.com › 54581-grapes-nutrition
Grapes: Health Benefits & Nutrition Facts | Live Science

Top Banana Producing Countries In The World. **India** produces the largest number of bananas in the world followed by **China** and **Philippines**. Apr 25, 2017

www.worldatlas.com › articles › top-banana-producing-c...
Top Banana Producing Countries In The World - WorldAtlas.com

The 20 Most Expensive Wines In the World

- Chateau Lafite 1787 – $156,450. ...
- Ampoule from Penfolds – $168,000. ...
- Chateau Margaux 1787 – $225,000. ...
- Chateau Lafite 1869 – $230,000. ...
- Shipwrecked 1907 Heidsieck – $275,000. ...
- Cheval Blanc 1947 – $305,000. ...
- Jeroboam of Chateau Mouton-Rothschild 1945 – $310,000. ...
- Screaming Eagle Cabernet 1992 – $500,000.

05-09 [_] Try to Imagine how many Billions of Dollars that you could Save in one Lifetime, just by Producing and Drinking your own Wine? I just Saved a Million Dollars TODAY, by not Drinking any! Someone Discovered an Old Sunken Ship with some Bottles of Wine, which Cost Millions of Dollars! We can make Better Wines for FREE! Drink all you Want, for FREE! †§‡

05-10 [_] O Great White Bald Eagle, it is just a simple Matter of CLAIMING our own Mountains of Rocks, Rivers of Water, Sand, Gravel, Clay, Minerals, Metals, and whatever we Need for True Prosperity; and then let the Edomites have whatever we do not Need nor Want, who are Welcome to Eat Snake Eggs, Poisonous Frogs, Mosquitoes, Ticks, Bedbugs, Lice, Fleas, or whatever they can Find in Abandoned Houses, Sewage Systems, and Used Condoms. After all, they are the People who Say that they do not have enough Money for Building those **"GLORIOUS Swanky Hotels Castles and Fortresses,"** which will Cost NOTHING, if we, the People, simply Elect YOU to be our Righteous KING! Moreover, when we get those Beautiful Planned City States Finished, we will simply MOVE INTO THEM, and tell the Fake Federal Government to go Straight to HELL! And all of the Righteous People will say a Hearty, "AMEN — let it be Done!" [_] Amen.

{FOOTNOTE: A Swanky Fortress that is 200 Miles by 200 Miles square can easily Service 100 Million People, if it is Managed Correctly. The State of Texas, alone, could Contain no less than 6 such Cities. Montana has Space for 2 more, and each of the States of Kansas, Nebraska, Iowa, South Dakota, North Dakota, Wisconsin, Missouri, Arkansas, Oklahoma, Wyoming, Utah, Arizona, Washington, Oregon, Idaho, California, Nevada, New Mexico, Mississippi, Alabama, Louisiana, Georgia, Florida, New York, Pennsylvania, Virginia, Tennessee, Illinois, Indiana, West Virginia, Kentucky, and Colorado have enough Space for no less than 40 of those Cities in smaller Sizes; or, roughly enough Space for 6 Billion People! So, that leaves all of South America, Mexico, Australia, China, Russia, Canada, and the Middle East for the Remaining 44 Billion People, who could easily be Fitted into Africa and Arabia, except that there is no Need for it: beCause we still have India, Indonesia, Malaysia, Japan, and other HUGE Countries to Populate, which only Require some Rearrangements of some Mountains of ROCKS, Sand, Gravel, Clay, Water and whatever. As many as 10 Families could Live in just one Stone Dome Home COMPLEX, Comfortably. For Example, I only Need a Small Space that covers 400 square feet. There are about 44,000 square feet in one Acre, which could contain no less than 50 such

Living Spaces, or roughly 40 People per Acre, which might seem to be a little Overcrowded, like Chickens in a Big Chicken House; but, they would be Sharing their Walk-in Coolers, Freezers, Root Cellars, Pantries, Large Living Rooms, Swimming Pools, Game Rooms, and whatever — not to mention the Joining Palaces with Churches, Truth-braries, Theaters, Concert Halls, Gymnasiums, Tennis Courts, Bowling Alleys, Ice-skating Rinks, Roller Skating Rinks, Museums, Craft Shops, Sales Shops, Factories, and whatever they Want or Need. All of the Buildings would be Under the Ground, and mostly Hidden from the Views to any Eagles, all Covered with All-Mineral Organic Gardens, Vineyards, Berry Bushes, Fruit Orchards, Nut Trees, and Flower Gardens, in Beautiful Patterns and Designs, being in Great Stone TERRACES. Everything would have to be Planned Properly for True Prosperity. All of the Transportation would be Underground in Electric Subway Trains, Elevators and Escalators, as well as Tiled Tunnels with Fish Aquariums and Bike Paths and Highways for Quadracycles going around on the Tops of the Terraced Walls, above the Arcades of Wind Funnels for FREE ElecTrickery, overlooking the many Beautiful Gardens and Fruit Trees. (See the Drawings below Verse 01-08.) End of Footnote.}

Those are Lime Trees, backed up by a Mango Tree, which is about 40 feet Tall.

— Chapter 06 —

How to STOP all Crimes!

06-01 [_] Just Check Out the following Statistics:

In 2018, the **US murder** rate was 5.0 **per** 100,000, **for a** total of 15,498 **murders.**

en.wikipedia.org › wiki › Crime_in_the_United_States
Crime in the United States - Wikipedia

What city in America has the lowest crime rate?

Simi Valley also **has** one of the **lowest** property **crime rates** of any U.S. **city** tracked by the FBI. There were only 1,172 property **crimes** like motor vehicle theft and burglary for every 100,000 people in 2018, nearly half the national property **crime rate** of 2,200 per 100,000. Oct 27, 2019

www.usatoday.com › story › money › 2019/10/27 › crim...
Crime rates are lower in these US cities with fewer ... - USA Today

Where is the best state to live?

Massachusetts

Massachusetts ranks as the **best state to live** in, in part due to its well-educated population. Nov 7, 2019

www.usatoday.com › story › money › 2019/11/07 › best-...
Massachusetts, Colorado, New Jersey among best US states to live in

06-02 [_] So, how many Crimes are committed in Massachusetts?

Massachusetts Annual Crimes

	Violent	Total
Number of **Crimes**	23,337	110,533
Crime Rate (per 1,000 residents)	3.38	16.01

www.neighborhoodscout.com › ma › crime ▼
Massachusetts Crime Rates and Statistics - NeighborhoodScout

06-03 |_| If you Discover a Criminal of any Kind at a Swanky Fortress, who cannot be Corrected by Love and a few School Lessons, you can have him Banished, whereby his Crimes will CEASE! However, just to Enter into a Swanky Fortress, everyone must Fill Out and File: **"The Complete SURVEYS of our VALUES!" (SURVEYS of Religious, Spiritual, Political, Governmental, Sexual, Social, Moral, Economical, Business, Labor, Habitual and Miscellaneous VALUES!) By The Worldwide People's Revolution!®** Book 059, whereby any Potential Thieves, Robbers, Liars, Rapists, Murderers, Adulterers, Wife Beaters, Husband Abusers, Child Abusers, Old People Abusers, and other Criminals can easily be Discovered: beCause of the Boxes that they have Checked. Therefore, the Worst People can be Sifted OUT, before they even Step one Foot into the Fortress. Moreover, some Fortresses will have Laws so Strict that Potential Criminals will not even Consider Entering into them; while others will be so Liberal that almost anyone will Want to Live within them. They will just have to Deal with whomever they Invite in, at their own Expenses. But, the Wise People will Choose to Live with ME, whereby there will be NO Crimes, NO Taxes, NO Slave Labor, NO Riots, NO Strikes, NO Bills, NO Poor People, NO Rich Hogs, NO Suicides, NO Unhappy Marriages, NO Divorces, NO Drugs, NO Snakes, NO Bedbugs, NO Fleas, NO Ticks, NO Mosquitoes, NO Lice, NO Mice, NO Mean People, NO Drug Addicts, NO Drugs for Sale, NO Prisons, NO Hospital Bills, NO Funeral Bills, NO Electric Bills, NO Gas Bills, NO Water Bills, NO Food Bills, NO Insurance Bills, NO Loans, NO Interest, NO Usury, and NO Wages: beCause, everything will be FREE! Moreover, everyone will be Welcome to Eat at one of thousands of **"Royal Swanky Buffets!" (The Best Feasts in the Whole World!) By The Worldwide People's Revolution!®** Book 103. Indeed, large Flat-screen TVs will be in every Dome Home Complex, in every Bedroom, Living Room, Kitchen, and Bathroom, if the People Want to Produce them, for FREE, which Means that a Person might have to Contribute 3 to 4 Hours of Common Skilled Labor to Help Produce them. Perhaps you could Pick a few Pints of Blueberries, to Trade for your Flat-screen TV? Indeed, even if you had to Pick 500 Pints, it would not Cost 3,000 Dollars for a 500-dollar Plastic TV, which might be Produced for as little as 20 Hours of Labor: beCause of Using Mechanical Slaves, Robots, and People who are Happy to Contribute their Time and Energy for such a Cause, just to have FREE TV Services, and no Internet Bills: beCause a Satellite Costs less than one-million Dollars, or 1 Penny per Person for 100-million People! So, why Pay 100-dollars per Month for a TV Service, which should be FREE? †§‡

How much does a 100 inch TV cost?

Hisense 100L10E 100-Inch 4K UHD Smart Laser Projector TV with Screen and 2.1 Audio System (2019)

List Price: **$8,999.99**

Price: $8,499.99 & FREE Shipping

Price. The Oyster Perpetual is the lowest priced model of **Rolex**. And it comes at a little over $5,000. May 13, 2019

06-04 [_] Notice that 999.99, which is only one Penny away from being 1,000 Dollars. Therefore, why not say that the TV Costs 9,000 Dollars? What is the Deception for? And then, the Capitalist Hogs add on some Sales Taxes, Service Agreements, Delivery Expenses, and so on, until it Actually Costs more than 10,000 Dollars! For Example, you have to have an Internet Connection with a Monthly Bill to Pay; but, not at any Swanky Fortress, once they are all Set Up Properly. Indeed, you would not OWN the TV, the Stone Dome Home Complex, nor even your 10,000-dollar Rolex Watch: beCause, you could simply go to the Tool House and get one, for FREE! And when you got Caught Selling it to someone who Lives OUTSIDE of your Fortress, your Ass would be Whipped with 30 Lashes, and you would be put to Work in a Rock Quarry for 10 Years, at HARD Labor: beCause of not Keeping your Promises to Act Civilized. Therefore, if you leave the Fortress with a Rolex Watch, you must Return with it, even if you Drop it into a Deep Well: beCause you do not have to take it with you when you Want to Show Off your Wealth, which is nothing but PRIDE. Awe, but, some Robbers could Rob your Rolex Watch, which is WHY that you did not Return with it, right? Well, the Great Question is this: **"WHY would you even Want to Leave a Swanky Fortress, to Visit any Idiots on the Outside?"** Answer, "You LOVE them, and Want to SAVE them!" Well, in that Case, just Send a Letter to them with some Pictures in it. E-mail them some Words and Pictures, whereby they can Decide if they Want to Live in any Crime-infested Cities of Confusion; or, Move their Lazy Asses into Beautiful Swanky Fortresses? Otherwise, we could get Really MEAN, and DRAFT them into a Mean Army of Murderous Soldiers, whereby they might GROW UP! Yes, they will call it World War 3: beCause that will be their Just Reward for Rejecting my Inspired Words of Provable Truths! Indeed, they could have all been Moderately RICH, with the True Riches, if they had been WISE, and Obeyed their Elected King; but, behold, if they Act like FOOLS, they will get the Rewards of FOOLS! Guaranteed! †§‡

06-05 [_] Only Criminals and Potential Criminals will Object to the Master Plan of the Colorful Peacock from Angel Ridge, who is Impersonating the Great White Bald Eagle: beCause that is something that he Does for the Glory of GOD, who Wants to Bless ALL People; but, only IF they Want to BE Blest: beCause he is not going to FORCE them to be Blest. Indeed, they have to Willingly CHOOSE to be Blest: beCause, it is like Joshua said, *"Choose you this Day whom you will Serve; but, as for me and my Household, we will Serve the Supreme Ruler, from whom all Good Blessings Come. Therefore, make up your Minds, and be Wise for yourselves, and Choose ALL that is GOOD: beCause that is GOD!" — Joshua something, NMV.*

06-06 [_] Do you See that "Million-dollar" Onyx Jewelry Box? There is a 10-million-dollar Gemstone in it. You can have the Box and the Gemstone, for FREE, if you can Prove my Inspired Words of Provable Truths to be WRong! Do not Try to Steal it: beCause the Penalty for that is to have your Hand Chopped OFF, unless you Quickly REPENT! It is the only Box in the entire World, which is just Exactly like the Picture, which is easy to Recognize. Trust me, any Thief will be Caught and Punished. There are 24/7/365 Guards, Security Cameras, Watch Dogs, and so on. Therefore, do not make a Fool of yourself. Likewise, when you Live in a Beautiful Swanky Palace, do not be Tempted to Steal anything: beCause you will be Caught. Indeed, the only Way into the Fortress System is through a very Long Spooky Tunnel, which has Traps Set Up for Catching Criminals, coming In or going Out; and some Fortresses have very Strict Laws, which will Prove to be Merciless Laws. Therefore, put all silly Temptations OUT of your Mind, and Think NO Evil: beCause it is Bad for your Good Health. After all, if you Want to be a Criminal of some Kind, just Stay in some City of Confusion, where it is Legal: beCause they Want you there; but, we do NOT.

06-07 [_] O Great White Bald Eagle, if you can Manage to Establish a Righteous One-World Government, all of those Thieves and Liars will simply Disappear: beCause no one will have any Justified CAUSE for Stealing, Lying, Robbing, Murdering, Raping, Committing Adultery, Sodomy, nor any other Forbidden Things: beCause they will all be Free to CHOOSE whatever they Want, even if they Sincerely Want to Steal, Rape, Rob, Murder or whatever: beCause there will be Places where it will be LEGAL, and they will be Welcome to Go there and Enjoy it! For Example, when all of the Righteous People ABANDON New York City, and Move into Swanky Fortresses, only Lawless Criminals will be Left in New Yuck City, who will soon Discover what it is Like to Live with Lawless People, who will soon be Inventing their own Laws and Regulations, just to keep from being Driven CRAZY by the Hordes of Criminals! †§‡

06-08 [_] Well, my Friend, it will not take those Remaining Criminals very long to Realize the NEED for Law and Order, whereby they will be Wanting to Hire some Marshal Matt Dillon to Straighten Things Out; but, there will be none to Hire: beCause they will have also Moved into Swanky Fortresses. Therefore, New Yuck City will be ABANDONED! Yes, it will Fulfill an Ancient Prophecy: *"There shall be many Great and Fair Cities of Confusion Laid Waste, without an Inhabitant: beCause all Cities of Confusion will be Abandoned."* — See: *Jeremiah 4:5—7.*

06-09 [_] O Great White Bald Eagle, that is not a Quotation from Jeremiah 4. Nevertheless, are you Sure that there are any RIGHTEOUS People Living in New Yuck City, at all? Are you Sure that the Atomic and Hydrogen Bombs will not have to be Used to get RID of them? After all, your Selected King is not Asking them to Abandon any GOOD Things; but, only Drugs, Tobacco Products, Stinking Perfumes, Makeup, Chemical Fertilizers, Polluting Vehicles, Paints, Solvents, Pesticides, Herbicides, Nuclear Power Plants, and all other Abominations. Therefore, a Person with his or her Riit Miind will simply Pack up his or her Rags in their Bags, and MOVE OUT! †‡

06-10 [_] Well, my Friend, that is easier Said than Done: beCause they have Friends and Relatives that they do not Want to Forsake. Therefore, it will be Like Father Abraham Departing from his own Family, and Moving to the Promised Land, which was a very Difficult Thing to Do. However, I Suggest that the Righteous Person should Remember LOT, who was the Nephew of Abraham, who Barely Escaped with his Life: beCause of Obeying the Holy Angels. After all, there are New Friends and Better Friends to be had in a Swanky Fortress. But, if you Love someone, and Want to Save their Soul, just Present a Copy of this Inspired Book to them, along with: **"Modern Deceived SLAVES!" (10 Simple Steps for Liberating ALL Slaves, Worldwide, Including Yourself!) By Liberty and Justice for ALL!** Book 113. Indeed, you do not have to Give Up all HOPE: beCause, just as long as they are Alive, there is Hope that they might also Escape to a Swanky Fortress, somewhere in the Wilderness. Therefore, be Diligent, and Study the Inspired Books of the Colorful Peacock from Angel Ridge, King's Mountain, Kentucky 40442 U.S.A.

{Mesa Verde in Colorado was the Home of Survivalists, who had no Bills to Pay.}

— Chapter 07 —

WHO is Worthy to Escape?

07-01 [_] Most Professing "Christians" Want to Escape from the Great Tribulation, and a few of them will even Confess that they have a Secret Plan for Doing that; but, none of them are quite Sure that they will Escape, in spite of the Fact that Jesus said, *"Pray that you are Accounted among the Worthy Ones to Escape,"* in *Luke 21:36;* or, as the *King James Version (KJV)* puts it: *"Watch ye therefore, and pray always, that ye may be accounted worthy to escape all these things that shall come to pass, and to stand before the Son of man."* {It is Suggesting that if you always Pray, you might Escape. So, the *New King James Version (NKJV)* makes an Attempt to Clarify it.} *"Watch therefore, and pray always that you may be counted worthy to escape all these things that will come to pass, and to stand before the Son of man."* Then the *New Living Translation* gets very Bold, and states: *"Keep alert at all times. And pray that you might be strong enough to escape these coming horrors and stand before the Son of man."* {If Strength were the Requirement for Escaping, those Body Builders might Escape; but, it Clearly states in *the Book of Revelation* that the True Church will *"... take the Wings of a Great Eagle, and Fly Away into the Wilderness, ..."* which seems to be Implying that they will Fly Away in an Airplane, which is most Likely. See *Revelation 11—13.*} The *New International Version* states: *"Be always on the watch, and pray that you may be able to escape all that is about to happen, and that you may be able to stand before the Son of Man."* I wonder WHO that Man is? They left Out a single Letter. It should read, *"... and to Stand Firmly in front of the Son of a Man,"* who was Joseph, the Father of Jesus, whose Special Seed was Transplanted from his Loins into the Womb of Mary by the Power of the Holy Spirit, while they both Slept in Separate Beds. Now, the *English Standard Version* takes up the Challenge to get a more-perfect Translation, which reads: *"But stay awake at all times, praying that you may have strength to escape all these things that are going to take place, and to stand before the Son of Man."* The *Christian Standard Bible* is almost a Copy of the English Standard Version, and it only changes the Stay Awake into Be Alert at all Times Attitude, which the Church has been Practicing for nearly 2,000 Years! But, "Wait a little Longer, and he is Bound to Return, whereby no one will have to Escape!" HUMBUG! I Prefer the New MAGNIFIED Version: "Watch the News, therefore, and always Pray to God: so that you might be Counted among the Righteous Ones, who are Worthy to Escape from all of those Evil Things that shall

Happen, if People do not Repent; and to Stand in front of the Chosen Son of a Holy Man in Mount Zion, who is going to Prepare a Special Place for you in that Great City of Refuge. Yes, her Palaces are known as a Place of Refuge, even a Place to Run to and Hide during Times of Great Troubles, just as it is Written in the Psalms." (See *Psalms 48, 50 and 87.*)

07-02 [_] O Great White Bald Eagle, you have a very Lofty View of Life and Death. Therefore, if anyone should Know just Exactly HOW and WHEN and WHERE the Church will Escape to, it should be YOU! But, WHO among us is WORTHY to Escape, seeing that we are all Sinners of Various Kinds and Colors, who are not making any Real Efforts to Overcome our Sins? ‡

07-03 [_] Well, my Friend, even if I Knew Exactly, I would not Reveal it within this Book: beCause this is just a Tale of Warning — not a Tale of Revelation, in spite of having a few dozen Revealing Things within it.

07-04 [_] O Great White Bald Eagle, why do you not just Watch the Evening News Reports, and Forget about Escaping from any Great Tribulation? After all, the Rollercoaster Economy will no doubt Continue to do its Rollercoasting, as Usual: beCause that is the Nature of Capitalism, Communism and Socialism, which are going UP and DOWN Continually: beCause of Playing the Money Game, while **"SWANGKEENOMIKS Rules the Roost!" (HOW all People can Prosper in a RIIT WAA, and STOP Polluting the Earth with Capitalist TRASH!) By The Worldwide People's Revolution!® Book 039**: beCause, Swankynomics provides a Way for everyone to get Set Up Properly for Living, at HOME, no matter what nonsense is taking place on Wall Street. ‡

07-05 [_] Well, my Friend, in the Capitalist Economic System, there is no Democracy at all: beCause the King in Charge of the Business is the "Tyrant" who makes all of the Decisions for his Slaves, who must Obey, or else get Fired! Therefore, for Capitalists to say that they Believe in Democracy is just a JOKE! So, are Greedy Selfish Capitalists Worthy to Escape from the Great Tribulation, and also from the Great ATOMIC NIGHTMARE, as a Result of Capitalist Mentality? NEVER: beCause they are the EVIL People, who Invented the Evils that Cause other Nations to HATE us — such as the Mountains of PLASTICS, for Example, which was an Economical Thing in the Minds of Capitalists, who made all such Trash to "save on money." Indeed, Capitalism never Asks, "Is this Product Harmful to People, Animals, the Environment, and the Earth?" But, they only Ask, "Is this Product PROFITABLE?" And, if it is Profitable for them, they Mass-produce it and Sell it, and Run to the Bank with the Profits: beCause that is what they are most-interested in. Therefore, if anyone Suggests that they should be Regulated by certain Laws, such a Person is Automatically an Enemy of Capitalism, which Means that they are SATANIC: beCause they Speak Evil of the Goddess called "Capitalism," who is Worshiped by all of the Moneymongers. ‡

07-06 [_] O Great White Bald Eagle, if the Christian Republicans, who Believe in Capitalism as the Economic Salvation of Mankind, will not Qualify to Escape from the Great Tribulation, nor from the Great ATOMIC NIGHTMARE, who will be Escaping?

07-07 [_] Well, my Friend, only the Elected Servants of God will Escape from the Great Tribulation; but, just anyone with some Brains in his Head could easily Escape from the Great Atomic Nightmare, just by MOVING to some less-threatened Place — such as Guatemala, Honduras, El Salvador, Costa Rica, Bolivia, Colombia, or to some other Poor Nation, even in Mexico, which has not been a Notorious Warmonger Nation, in spite of Buying into the Capitalist Scam, whereby they have only a few Rich Hogs, and Hordes of Extremely Poor People, and a Middle Class that has few Bills to Pay: beCause of Practicing Socialism, and beCause of Living in a Mild Climate, which Eliminates Heating and Cooling Bills, for Example. Foods are also much Cheaper in Mexico: beCause of the Mild Climate, and Hordes of Poor People, who are Willing to Work for almost nothing: beCause Capitalism cannot Afford to Pay them Good Wages. †§‡§§

07-08 [_] O Great White Bald Eagle, it is Obvious that only the Most-Righteous People will Escape from all of the Evils that will come onto the Wicked People: beCause, only the Righteous People are Worthy to Escape, which Excludes most People, including the Poorest and most-Humble People, who will have no Means for Escaping, who cannot Afford "the Wings of a Great Eagle," you might say. In Fact, they do well to Afford to EAT. Therefore, it is Obvious that Jesus was Addressing his Messages to a Select FEW Israelites, only, who may be Modern Americans; but, I Doubt it: beCause they do not Act like the Disciples of Jesus Christ, except for a Select FEW. †§‡

07-09 [_] Well, my Friend, you bring up an Interesting Subject, which concerns WHO we ARE, and what we should Believe, or not Believe. However, as a True Christian, a Believer must Accept the Doctrines and Teachings of Jesus Christ, who Obviously Tawt the Doctrine of COMMONISM; or of having ALL MATERIAL THINGS IN

COMMON, which was Practiced by the First Church of Jesus Christ in *the Book of Acts,* which is not Practiced by most so-called "Believers" during these Days: beCause that would not be "Profitable," they say. But, at the same Time, most of those Professing "Christians" will Confess that LOVE is Good, even if it is not Profitable for the Devil, who Loves Wars, Crimes, Poverty, Sicknesses, Diseases, Famines, and all Kinds of Evils. †§‡

07-10 [_] O Great White Bald Eagle, do you Think that your Selected King's Economic System should be FORCED onto the Masses of People?

— Chapter 08 —

Should an Economic System, which has been Proven to be Good, be Forced onto People?

08-01 [_] First of all, I want to make it Clear that I am NOT a Communist, a Capitalist, nor a Socialist, much less, a Fascist; but, I am a Firm Believer in Liberty and JUSTICE for ALL Peoples, even if they are Communists, Capitalists, Socialists, Fascists, or whatever, who should be Free to Practice whatever Insane Economic System that they might Like, just as long as it does not Destroy the Earth in any Way, which is Subject to Various Interpretations. Nevertheless, if any one of those Economic Systems were Truly GOOD, almost anyone should be Able to Prove it. Sorry to say, they are all Bad: beCause there is only ONE Economic System that has Zero Faults, and it is called: Swangkeenomiks in Phonetic English, which is Based on the Garden of Eden Plan, whereby everyone is Set Up Properly for Living, at Home, whereby they are not Dependent on Selling anything. Indeed, if they Need or Want more Money, they can Work for **"The New RIGHTEOUS One-World Government,"** which has an Endless Supply of Good Money, which must be Earned by Honest Labor, doing something that is Good and Necessary — such as Building Swanky Cisterns for Water Storage: beCause it is Impossible to have too much Fresh Living Water, which can be Produced at Swanky Fortresses, which is Explained in other Inspired Books. ‡

08-02 [_] O Great White Bald Eagle, if the Swanky Economic System has been Proven to be very GOOD, why not just FORCE People to Accept it and Practice it? For Example, when you Live and Work at Home, in your All-Mineral Organic Garden, or in your Home-craft Workshop with Well-made Tools, you can go Shopping at HOME, in your own Garden, Walk-in Cooler / Freezer, Pantry, or Root Cellar; but, if you are Missing some Special Spices, or something that is Grown in some other Country, you can Trade some Money for it, if you Want to. Otherwise, you could simply Eat at a Royal Swanky Buffet, and let **"The Swanky Association of Professional Organic Gardeners"** take Care of the Gardening: beCause they would also Fill your Pantry with thousands of Jars of Delicious Foods, just to make Sure that you can Survive and Thrive, which no other Economic System even Proposes: beCause they are all Slavery Systems, which Require 8 to 16 or more Hours of Work, just to Barely Survive: beCause of all of those Endless BILLS to Pay! †§‡

08-03 [_] Well, my Friend, when some Government FORCES the People to Do whatever they do not Want to Do, they become Rebellious, just for the Sake of being Stubborn, if for nothing else. Indeed, they say, "Give to me Liberty; or, Give to me DEATH!" And they are Serious about that: beCause they should be Free to Choose whatever they Want, which they would be, in the Swanky Fortress System, which only Requires that they Choose to Live with Like-minded People: beCause we cannot Expect People, who are Like Sheeps and Goats, to get along Well with other People, who are Like Lions and Wolves: beCause they have Contrary Natures. Therefore, they should be kept SEPARATED by **"The New RIGHTEOUS One-World Government,"** Book 056, which is WHY that everyone should Fill Out and File: **"The Complete SURVEYS of our VALUES,"** Book 059, whereby we might Discover WHO is WHO! Moreover, no matter what you Believe, it is Okay, if your Beliefs are Harmless. In Fact, you can Keep all of the Weapons that you Want, in Order to DEFEND your Beliefs with other People of Like-mindedness, if you can Discover any.‡

08-04 [_] O Great White Bald Eagle, I am Glad that you are a Believer in the *Second Amendment* for the Constitution of the United States: beCause, we cannot Trust any Government, including **"The New RIGHTEOUS One-World Government!" (HOW to Establish a Righteous One-World Government without Going to WAR!) By The Worldwide People's Revolution!®** Book 056. Indeed, such a Monster Government might Turn Against us, and make Slaves of us. §‡

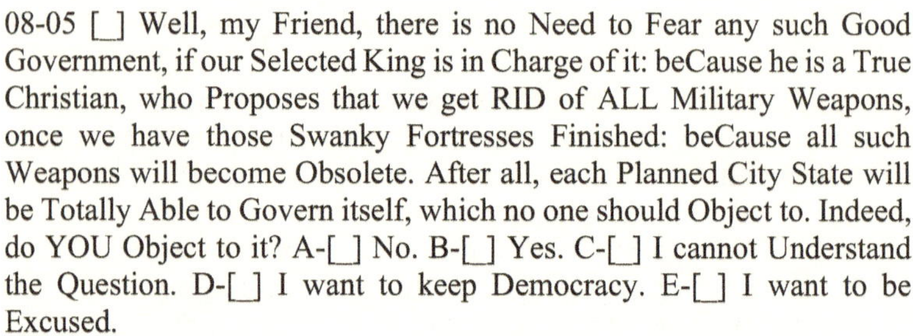

08-05 [_] Well, my Friend, there is no Need to Fear any such Good Government, if our Selected King is in Charge of it: beCause he is a True Christian, who Proposes that we get RID of ALL Military Weapons, once we have those Swanky Fortresses Finished: beCause all such Weapons will become Obsolete. After all, each Planned City State will be Totally Able to Govern itself, which no one should Object to. Indeed, do YOU Object to it? A-[_] No. B-[_] Yes. C-[_] I cannot Understand the Question. D-[_] I want to keep Democracy. E-[_] I want to be Excused.

08-06 [_] O Great White Bald Eagle, what your Selected King Proposes is TRUE Democracy, where everyone is Free to Choose whatever he or she Wants; but, only with other People of Like-mindedness: beCause People must be Able and Willing to get Along with each other. Therefore, Democrats should not be Mixing themselves with Republicans: beCause they do not get Along very Well. †§‡

08-07 [_] Well, my Friend, in the Swanky Fortress System, there is no Need for any Political Parties: beCause they are all Proven to be Ridiculous and Useless. After all, your Fruit Trees will not Care what your Political Beliefs might be; but, only what your Gardening Beliefs might be. And the Righteous One-World Government will do its Best to Help everyone to Do GOOD Gardening: beCause that is one of its Basic Duties: beCause it will Require a LOT of Experimenting, just to Discover what the Best Methods are, and without Inventing nor Using any Unnatural Poisons. In other Words, the Gardening must be Natural and Harmless. But, if anyone Objects to that Plan, they should Live with the Ignorant Fools, and Eat all of the Poisons that they Want, and Die with Cancers of Various Kinds, which is WHY that Fools should be Allowed to Use Tobacco Products; but, only in Cities of Confusion with other Ignorant Fools. ‡

08-08 [_] O Great White Bald Eagle, will the New RIGHTEOUS One-World Government be Collecting Taxes, for the Purpose of Treating the Victims of Capitalism, who have been Smoking, Eating Poisons, Drinking Abominations, or whatever, who have gotten Diseases?

08-09 [_] NO, absolutely NOT: beCause their Health is their Problem, if they Rebel against whatever Science has Proven — such as the Evilness of Smoking. Therefore, all such Smokers should Tax themselves. Likewise, People who Eat Unnatural Foods, which make them Sick, should Pay for their own Health Care: beCause those Bills should not be Covered by Righteous People, who Eat Natural Wholesome Foods, only, and in Moderation. Therefore, each Swanky Fortress will have the Responsibility of Providing its own Health Care. Therefore, if you do not Like Taxes, just Choose to Live with other Wise People, and you will not have any Taxes to Pay.

08-10 [_] O Great White Bald Eagle, who will be Responsible for Cleaning Up all of the Radioactive DUST after the Great ATOMIC NIGHTMARE?

♦ — Chapter 09 — ♦

Who will be Responsible for Cleaning Up the Radioactive Dust after the Great Atomic Nightmare?

09-01 [_] I fully Expect that 200 American Cities will be BOMBED, just to Reap 100-fold for Sowing 2 Mean Seeds in Japan, on Hiroshima and Nagasaki, in 1945, after Firebombing more than 10,000 Villages and Cities with Napalm Bombs: beCause those are the Kinds of Evil Deeds that American Leaders Do in the Names of Freedom, Liberty, and Justice for ALL: beCause, "they are God's Chosen People," according to Edgar Allan Poe and Sir Winston Cigar-chomping Whiskey-guzzling Churchill, who could have been the Reincarnation of Edgar: beCause he had a "Dark Mysterious Mind," while Adolf Hitler had a Clear and Brilliant Mind as a Politician, Orator and Manipulator, who has the Reputation of a Mass Murderer: beCause of the Edomite Propaganda Machine, which has never Reported the Whole Truth about the Evil Events of the 20th Century: beCause those Lying Conniving Edomites have their own Special Agenda, even as they always have had, ever since they Orchestrated the Death of the Most-Righteous Man who ever Lived, and Blamed it onto the Romans, rather than Accept Full Responsibility for it, themselves, even as they Blamed Osama bin Laden for the Evil Events of September 11th, 2001, when he had Absolutely NOTHING to Do with it; but, he made a Good Patsy, even as Lee Harvey Oswald made a Good Edomite Patsy for the Assassination of President John F. Kennedy, who was the Victim of another Edomite Scandal, with Lyndon Baines Johnson in Charge of it, which you can Discover on a YouTube Video, called: **Kennedy: A Legacy in Blood — the Final Chapter — "Johnson — (The Head of the Snake)"** which goes into all of the Gory Details, and Concludes that Part of History. But, the HoloHOAX Part of

History has yet to be Concluded in a Courtroom, with an Honest Judge and Jury in Charge of it: beCause the Edomites Control the Propaganda Machines, you might say, which is a Primary Reason for the Hydrogen and Atomic Bombs to Fall on THEM, in New Yuck City, Washington, District of Chief Criminals, and in the Land of Israel, where Fake Jews have Gathered like Vultures and Buzzards, along with many Innocent Lost Sheeps, who have no Idea HOW that they have been Deceived by the Edomites, who are a Mixture of Israelites and Edomites, which is WHY that they were Called "JEWS," to begin with: beCause the Edomites Interbred with the Tribes of Judah, Levi and Benjamin, in Order to Obtain the Leadership in the Land of Israel: beCause the Edomites, who were Descendants of Esau, who was the Twin Brother of Jacob, were Determined to get as much MONEY as Possible, by Capitalizing on the Israelite Bible, which they EDITED, about 400 Years before the Time of Christ, when they Lived in Babylon, at which Time they also Invented Biblical Stories to Enhance the Bible, and make it a Sellable Book: beCause the Edomites were very Intellectual People, and still are, until this very Day: beCause that is their GIFT from Satan, as Jesus Explained in *the Gospel of Saint John,* and also in *the Book of Revelation,* where Jesus tells John that those Edomites are of the Synagogue of Satan, who Call themselves JEWS; but, they are NOT Israelites. (See Chapters 2:9 and 3:9, which is Amazingly Revealing, and just Barely got put into the Book. In Fact, the entire Book of Revelation just Barely got Voted into the *Holy Bible,* when the 66 Books were Approved by the Edomites, in 1611.) In Fact, the Israelites are LIKE Jacob in many Ways, who are rather Simple-minded People, while the Edomites are somewhat Like LABAN, who was Jacob's Father-in-law, who Changed Jacob's Wages 7 Times: beCause he was another Edomite, at Heart. Indeed, Jacob Married into that same Family that Isaac had Married into, whereby his Wife Sarah gave Birth to those Twins, and Esau turned out to be a Murderer and Liar in his Heart, while Jacob turned out to be a Good Person at Heart, which was also True for most of his 12 Sons; but, especially for Joseph and Benjamin, who were Special Sons — at least According to the Stories, which could be True for the most Part; but, those Stories have yet to be Proven in a Courtroom with Law and Order. Indeed, one hardly Dares to Question anything that is Biblical: beCause, "It is the Word of GOD," they say, whereby that False Saying has been Greatly Enhanced by Zealous Preachers, who say: "The Holy Bible is the Inerrant, Infallible, and Inspired Word of the Living God," as if it were only ONE Word, "which is JESUS," they say, who is "The Word of God in the Flesh," according to *John 1.* Well, Possibly so; but, who would Know for Sure: beCause of the Fact that the Edomites Carefully EDITED the entire Bible, before they Published it, a few hundred Years after the Time of Christ, when they Selected the Books that they Wanted Published, while Deleting the thousands of Manuscripts that they did NOT Want Published, lest some of the Children should Read those Manuscripts, and come to Realize the FRAUDULENT HOAX that was being Played on them, in the Name of GOD, who was Winking at all of it: beCause he Understood Exactly what was Happening! In Fact, God Allowed it for a Good Purpose, whereby he might Discover the Honest and Reliable People, whom he would make Future Rulers in his Great Kingdom: beCause he Knew that all such Honest People would be Able to Sense the Whole Truth when they got to Hear it, at whatever Time that they might get to Hear it: beCause they have the Sixth Sense, which is to Sense the TRUTH! †§‡

www.towncaredental.com › blog › what-substances-ma... ▾
What Substances Make Up Your Teeth? | Affordable Dental ...
Jul 15, 2015 - Enamel is the hardest substance in the human body, and it covers the outer surface of your **teeth**. It is **made** mostly of an extremely hard mineral ...

09-02 [_] O Great White Bald Eagle, I Sense that you are in Business to Sell another Pack of Anti-Semitic LIES, which are Aimed at Destroying the HOLOCAUST Myth, which is Actually a True Story, which can be Proven in a Courtroom, when all of the Evidences are Presented for our Careful Inspection. For Example, any Honest Caretaker of a Crematory Oven will Confess that it Requires no less than 4 Hours to Cremate a Human Body, even if it is only a little Baby of a Couple of Years of Age: beCause it has TEETH, and all Teeths are made of very HARD MINERALS, which Require TIME to Burn Up and make into Ashes, which can take as much as 8 to 12 Hours for an Old Man, even at Extremely HOT Temperatures in a Crematory Oven! However, those Lying Conniving Edomites clearly state that those Wicked Nazis put 4 to 6 Bodies into Nazi Ovens every few Minutes, in Mixtures of Baby Bodies and Adult Bodies, which anyone can Discover on the Internet. For Example, here are some of their Confessions:

How many cremation ovens are in Auschwitz? ⌃

By the early spring of 1943, four huge crematoria became fully operational at Auschwitz II (Birkenau). They housed eight gas chambers and forty-**six ovens** that could dispose of some 4,400 corpses per day.

www.pbs.org › auschwitz › killing
Auschwitz: Inside the Nazi State . Auschwitz 1940-1945 . The Killing ...

09-03 [_] So, O Great White Bald Eagle, if you Divide 4,400 by 46, it equals about 95 Bodies in just one Oven per Day, or one Body every 15 Minutes. (Just Divide 1,440 Minutes in one 24-hour Day by 95, and you get about 15 Minutes per Body.) In other Words, if it Required an Average of 6 Hours to Cremate one Adult, there must have been no less than 16 Bodies in one Oven, in Order to Cremate 95 Bodies in that Oven during one Day. (There cannot Possibly be any Exaggerations in the Google Search Engine. You can Trust every Word: beCause, it is also "the Word of God.") †§‡§§

How many died in Auschwitz per day?

From August to October 1942, 1.32 million Jews were either slain in Nazi **death** camps or shot in close by regions, an almost inconceivable 15,000 **people per day**, a new study suggests. Jan 2, 2019

www.usatoday.com › story › news › world › 2019/01/02
Holocaust deaths: 15,000 murdered per day in Aug.-Oct. 1942

09-04 [_] When you Multiply those 15,000 Bodies times 365 Days per Year, times 2 Years of Exterminations, you get 10,950,000 Bodies, or roughly 60% of the entire Jewish Population in the Whole World, which left about 4 Million Jewish Women of all Ages Remaining Alive, half of whom were either too Old to give Birth, or too Young to give Birth; but, the Amazing Thing is the Fact that those 2 Million Qualified Jewish Mothers Suddenly gave Birth to 9 Million Babies! And the Reason that I say that, is beCause the World Almanac Reported a Total of 19.5 Million Jews in the Whole World in 1940, and a Total of 17.5 Million Jews in 1950! Therefore, if 10,950,000 Jews were Murdered, or just Died during the HoloHOAX, that would have left only about 8 Million Jews in the Whole World by 1945, at the End of the War; and only half of those Jews were Womb-men; and only half or less of those were Eligible to get Pregnant! Therefore, it was another Biblical "MIRACLE," whereby only 2 Million Women gave Birth to about 8 Million Babies, in only 5 Years! Yes, they were having Quadruplets and Twins by the Dozens! — except that there are no Hospital Records of it, and no Birth Certificates to Prove it! Moreover, Jews are Notoriously Slow about having Children, at all, even Today, when the Average Jewish Growth Rate is about 1.2 Children during a Lifetime! But, it was not the Case during nor after the HoloHOAX: beCause it was a Time of Great Jewish Miracles, which began with the Deaths of only 168,000 Jews, according to the Red Cross, which the News Reporters quickly Exaggerated into 400,000 by the Time the News reached Wall Street, which was Revised to 800,000 within a Month or so; and was quickly Revised again to

1,200,000 within another Month or 2; and then, lo and behold, within a few Years it was 6 Million Victims of the Nazis, which Stuck at that Number for some 40 Years, or more, which was Revised again, just a few Years Ago, when more Evidences were Revealed by a Liar, who Conveniently Died before he could be brought into any Courtroom, which Raised the Death Toll to 11 Million, which would have been more than HALF of all Jews in the entire World, including those in China, India, Iran, Iraq, Jordan, Lebanon, Brazil, Argentina, Australia, New Zealand, Venezuela, Ecuador, Peru, South Africa, the United States of America, Canada, and wherever Jews had been Scattered Out during the past 2,000 or more Years. Granted, there was a Concentration of them in Europe, Russia and in other Communist Countries over there; but, not nearly ALL of the Jews had even been Rounded Up by those Wicked Nazis: beCause my own Great GREAT Grandparents were Living in Germany for the entire Time of the War Game, as Farmers, and no one even Bothered them, nor Asked them any Questions — much less, Haul them Off to any Concentration Camps: beCause Farmers were Needed for the War Effort as much as Weapons Manufacturers, most of whom were JEWS! Yes, you have to be Above Average Intelligence, just to be in that Kind of a Business, whereby Jews Fit the Requisition: beCause they were always Above Average Intelligence, even as they still are, until this very Day! For Example, I am one of them! — except that I am one of the HONEST Jews, like Benjamin Freedman: beCause I Firmly Believe in being Perfectly HONEST about ALL Things, including WHO Assassinated President Kennedy, and WHO Set Up the EXPLOSIVES that brought Down the World Trade Center (WTC) Towers during September 11th, 2001, along with the Assistance of Microwave Energy, according to Dr. Judy Wood. (Google her.) †§‡§§

09-05 [_] For Example, that Tall Hardened Steel Column was CUT OFF by a Common Hacksaw, which left the Molten Metal Dripping at the Bottom of the 45-degree Angled Cut: beCause the Big Fat Momma, who was Running the Hack Saw, was in a BIG Hurry to get it Done, before she gave Birth to that Edomite LIE — that TERRORISTS from Saudi Arabia Cut it Off with their Hard James Bond Teeths! But, of course, no one in his Riit Mind would Believe any such Jewish Fairy Tales, even if they were Repeated a million Times per Day on all Television Networks, Worldwide: beCause a lot of Gums would Naturally be Bleeding the Truth of it, and Bleeding all over the *Holy Bible,* also: beCause it was Prophesied by Isaiah and Jeremiah in *the Book of Ezekiel,* in Chapter 38, which is telling about the Great ATOMIC NIGHTMARE, as well as the Evil Events of September 11th, 2001, World Wars 1 and 2, plus other Major World Events — such as Men Walking on the Moon in their Night Gowns! Yes, the *Holy Bible* is Full of all Kinds of PROPHECIES, including several Chapters about Telegraphs, Telephones, Radios, Televisions, Radars, Submarines, Cars, Trucks, Buses, Trains, Airplanes, iPhones and COMPUTERS: beCause those Holy Prophets Knew about all such Things in Advance, which is Obvious by the FACT that they did not Mention even ONE of those Things that I just now Listed! In Fact, if you could Find even ONE Clear Prophecy within the entire *Holy Bible,* you might have a Justified Cause for Believing those Lying Conniving Edomites! But, behold, there is not so much as ONE Clear Prophecy about ANYTHING! For Example, Saint Peter could have written, *"And behold, it shall come to pass during the Last Days,*

just before the Second Coming of Jesus Christ in all of his Naked Glory, that Millions of People will be Flying around the World in Great Ships that look somewhat like BIRDS, or Long Large Serpents with Wings and Tails, which Transport hundreds of People at one Time." But, behold, there are no such Words in your Unholy Mutilated Bible: beCause neither Peter, James, John, nor the Apostle Paul Foreseen any such Things; or else, they Did See them, and Recorded them, and then the Lying Conniving Edomites EDITED THEM OUT! However, they Deny it; and they could be Right about that: beCause it is very Unlikely that ANY of the so-called "Holy Prophets" were Actually PROPHETS! Yes, MuhamMAD was another so-called "Holy Prophet," who never gave so much as ONE Clear Prophecy about ANYTHING! But, just to make Sure that no one Doubts me, I will now give to you a Clear and Precise PROPHECY, which will Come to Pass, whereby there will be no Doubt about it in the Mind of anyone who can Think and Remember! Therefore, SIT UP and Pay Strict Attention, O Lady Doubtfulness: beCause this is very Important! †§‡§§

09-06 |_| It shall come to Pass during the Process of Time — God only Knows just Exactly WHEN — that all of these Inspired Words of Provable Truths will go forth among the Children of Unholy Men, who will be Sick of Hearing all such Outlandish Jewish LIES, and will thus DEMAND: **"The GREAT Worldwide TELEVISED Court HEARING!" (That Great Meeting of the Most-Intelligent and Well-Educated Minds!) By The Worldwide People's Revolution!®** Book 041B, whereby they might Discover the Whole Truth and nothing but the Whole Truth, including the Whole Truth about the so-called "Jewish Holocaust," which is nothing more than a Great EXAGGERATION of the FACTS — such as those Gas Chambers, and the Murders of 15,000 Jews during just one Day, and every Day, for 2 Years, whereby so many MILLIONS of Jews might be Cremated ALIVE in Kitchen Stoves, after being Run through Nazi Crematory Ovens by the Dozens, which Reduced them to mere Bones and Teeths within 6 Minutes, after which those Bones and Teeths were put into Kitchen Ovens, all over Germany: beCause they were Transported by Drones in little Boxes, which were then Placed into those Ovens in every German Kitchen: beCause that was Possible, in spite of being Highly Unlikely, even as it was Highly Unlikely that anyone was Gassing 15,000 Jews to Death, each Day, just before no less than 30,000 Holocaust Survivor Books were Published with the Explicit Words: "I saw 2 great smoking chimneys at Auschwitz," or some Words that were very Similar to that, which Mentioned those 2 Great Smoking Chimneys in those Published Books, and no less than 2,689,054 Times! Yes, it is Astounding Information, when you Think about it with a Capital T! HOW in the World, or not in the World, could more than 30,000 Authors get it WRong? Were they ALL Telling LIES? Absolutely NOT! They were Telling the TRUTH, which they got from Eye Witnesses, themselves! Yes, everyone, including my own Grandparents, could Remember those 2 Great Smoking Chimneys at Auschwitz / Birkenau, Poland: beCAUSE they were Stinking Smoking Crematory Chimneys; but, not all of the Time! Yes, they were also LARGE Chimneys; but, any Crematory Engineer will quickly Confess that a Crematory Oven Requires a certain Amount of AIR, just for the Furnace to BURN; and all of that Stinking SMOKE must have a certain Amount of SPACE in a Chimney, in Order to VENT the Oven Properly, or else it will CHOKE OUT the Fire, and make MORE Smoke and Less Space for the Smoke to Exhaust itself, whereby the Fire will not Burn Properly, and the Oven will not even get HOT! In Fact, one large Chimney at Auschwitz could only Handle a Maximum of 5 Ovens at any given Time: beCause they were not Designed for 46 Ovens. Moreover, the Communist Russians flew Reconnaissance Missions over Auschwitz on a Regular Basis, in Order to Obtain Ariel Photographs to Study; and guess what? — they Obtained THOUSANDS of Testimonies in the Form of PHOTOGRAPHS of those 2 Great Smoking Chimneys! Yes, all such Photographs will be Presented at **"The GREAT Worldwide TELEVISED Court HEARING,"** just for the Sake of anyone who might Doubt my PROPHECY! After all, "Seeing is Believing" in this Case: beCause the Russians had no Reason for making up any Fake Photographs of Auschwitz to Study; nor would they Dare Destroy any such Photographs, after Showing them to the Investigators of the History Channel, whereby that Evidence was Reported all around the World! Indeed, it is NO Lie at all: beCause there was no Reason for Lying, even as those Eye Witnesses at Auschwitz had no Good Reason for Lying about those "2 Great Smoking Chimneys," beCause everyone Saw them! Therefore, the Great Question is: "WHO is now LYING to us?" †§‡§§

09-07 |_| There is very little Doubt about just Exactly WHO the Chief Liars ARE, and they have been Identified as EDOMITES! But, all such Lies and Liars must be STOPPED, before they Create another Real HOLOCAUST for themselves, called: **"The Great ATOMIC NIGHTMARE!" (The Saddest Story in World History!) By The Great White Bald Eagle!** Book 099. Yes, it will Happen, unless we, the People, STOP IT from Happening by DEMANDING **"The GREAT Worldwide TELEVISED Court HEARING,"** whereby the Record can be Set Straight — and, not only about that one very Important Subject; but, also about a thousand and one other very Important

Subjects — such as the Moon-landing HOAX, the False Flag Operations of World War 2, the Truth about Vietnam, the Oklahoma City Bombing, and many other HOAXES, which must be Proven, one Way or the other Way at that Great Meeting of the Most-Intelligent and Well-Educated Minds: beCause all of those Lies are Causing a GREAT DIVISION among Americans and other Nations, which Need to be EXPOSED in the Bright Shining Light of Provable Truths! Therefore, if you Agree with me about all of that, please place your LARGE GREEN-X MARK in the Above Box, and Confirm it by Checking this Box [ ] likewise. And Remember this: IF anyone Fails to Check those Boxes with a Positive X-mark, such a Person is Suspect of being an ENEMY of some Perverse Kind: beCause there is nothing at all EVIL about Conducting a COURT HEARING concerning any given CRIME, including the Crimes that took Place during September 11th, 2001, which was not even brought to COURT! In Fact, not one Aspect of it was brought to Court: beCause it was another Federal COVER-UP, like the Kennedy Assassination, which was also not brought to Court, whereby hundreds of Eye Witnesses did not get to Testify in any Courtroom, in spite of having much Evidence to Present to an Honest Jury, whereby the Real Criminals got by with First Degree MURDER! However, the Good News is the Fact that we can NOW Demand that Court Hearing, and get some True JUSTICE in only ONE Respect, which is to Hear the Whole Truth, whatever it might be; and I do not Personally Care what it might be: beCause I have already Drawn Up my own Godly Conclusions — namely, that those Lying Conniving Edomites are GUILTY as Charged! However, it is Possible and most Practical for them to REPENT, and Confess all of their Lies, and Escape from any Great Atomic Nightmare! However, if they will NOT Confess their Lies, those Communist Russians and Chinese have Agreed to BOMB THE HELL OUT OF THEM! Yes, they will not just Drop one nor 2 Bombs; but, 200 or more of them, just to Repay the Debts that we Americans Owe to them for all of the Lies that were Told to them, and for all of the Evils that were Done to them, both in Secret and in the Open. For Example, the Americans and Brits Promised Saint Joseph Stalin that they would Help him to Defeat those Wicked Nazis, while Americans and Brits were Financially Supporting those Nazis! Yes, it is an Extremely Complicated Subject: beCause that is a Typical Edomite Tactic, which gets most People CONFUSED, whereby they do not even Want to Think about it; nor should they have to Think about it: beCause it is like Studying the Logbook of Satan, himself, which is Full of Confusion and Contradictions: beCause he is the Chief Author of Confusion, and the Inventor of all such Edomite Lies. Therefore, when we Conduct that Great Meeting of the Most-Intelligent and Well-Educated Minds, we will

TRY to keep it all as Simple as Possible, by having those Edomites make their Clear Confessions, without Digging into the Edomite Poop that might be Found on the Tables in front of them, which no one will Want to Feast on for Weeks at a Time! In other Words, if they come Clean, and make their Full Confessions, beginning with Larry Silverstein, Rudely Jewleeonee, George Warmonger Bush, and Little Dick Chicanery, Incorporated, we can Clear Up that Subject during just ONE Day, which will Prove to be a bit Shocking to most Deceived Americans; but, not to the Victims of Capitalism, who have Studied: **"Modern Deceived SLAVES!" (10 Simple Steps for Liberating ALL Modern Slaves, Worldwide, Including Yourself!) By Liberty and Justice for ALL!** Book 113. †§‡§§

09-08 |_| Well, my Friend, I would say that whomever Reads this Inspired Book, and Fails to Check the Appropriate Boxes with his or her X-Marks, is Suspect of being an ENEMY, and a First-Class Enemy, who should be Summoned to COURT, and Tried for TREASON, even if his Name is Donald Trump, who should be the First in Line to DEMAND: **"The GREAT Worldwide TELEVISED Court HEARING,"** if he were Seeking the Whole Truth about anything, which, of course, he is NOT: beCause he is Obviously an Adopted Son of those Lying Conniving Edomites! Yes, that is WHY that he gave to them a Big TAX BREAK, if ye Recall, for which they no doubt Thanked him a lot; but, the Poor Abused Tax Slaves got their Appeasement or Pacification Checks, whereby they might be BRIBED into Keeping MUM with Poor Nigger Jim and Huck Finn, who have no Intentions of DEMANDING any Great Meetings of the Most-Intelligent and Well-Educated Minds: beCause they are Sure that they do NOT Want to Move into any **"Beautiful Swanky PALACES!" (A New Concept in Living Habits — Swanky Palaces for Poor People!) By The Worldwide People's Revolution!®** Book 066. In Fact, they just Want to go on Suffering in their Miserable States of Endless DEBTS and BILLS to Pay: beCause, they LOVE their SLAVERY! Yes, they also Love their Slave Masters, which is WHY that they never Speak Evil of Rich Edomite Bankers, Medical Snakes, Wicked Lawyers, nor Unjust Judges: beCause they FEAR to make Enemies of them. However, a New Day is Dawning, my Friends, and the Tables of the Money Changers are about to be Overturned, in spite of the Tables being a Million Times as HEAVY as they were during the Time of Christ, and Covered with Edomite Propagandist Lies, and in all Major Languages! †§‡§§

09-09 |_| O Great White Bald Eagle, it Required a little Time for you to get your Wings of Faith Warmed Up; but, then you went Soaring High into the Dark Awesome Rolling Clouds of a FEARSOME Sky, whereby you got me Lost and Confused: beCause I have not Studied the 112 other Inspired Books that you or some Good Friend has Written. Indeed, if there is a Great Atomic Nightmare, it will only be beCAUSE of those Edomites not Cooperating with **"The Swanky Sword of Divine Truths!" (The Most-Powerful Weapon in the Whole Universe!) By The Worldwide People's Revolution!®** Book 067. Therefore, the Wise Thing for them to Do, is to be the FIRST to Demand that Great Meeting of the Most-Intelligent Minds, whereby they can Control it, and Manipulate it for their own Gain: beCause they have everything to Gain by it, and nothing to Lose by it. In Fact, if they are Smart, they will Obtain **"The Great World TEMPLE of PEACE,"** in Jerusalem, whereby they can Return to the Good Old Days of King Solomon, who Established PEACE throughout all of the Lands, from Libya to Iran, and from South Africa to Great Britain, which used to be called Tarshish, where Jonah was Fleeing to, when he got Swallowed by a Hungry Whale Shark with a Fake Tale of Edomite Lies! After all, there is no Way in this World that 7 Billion People will REPENT of all of their Sins, nor Change their Ways of Thinking and Living, just beCause of Larry Silverstein making a Confession about the False Flag Operations of September 11th, 2001: beCause it was Orchestrated by Osama bin Laden and Sons, Incorporated. Yes, everyone Knows that, and Believes it to be the Whole Truth: beCause they have not Studied a YouTube Video, called: †§‡§§ **"Experts Speak Out!" (The 9/11/2001 False Flag Operation has Finally been Resolved!) By The Worldwide People's Revolution!®** Book 365.

09-10 [_] Well, my Friend, there still Remains a LOT of *Unsolved Mysteries,* as Robert Stack might say it; but, we are all getting Closer to the Great Judgment Day, when nothing will be Top Secret any longer. Therefore, just have Faith in God, who is All that is GOOD, and do not let go of the Strong *Rope of Hope:* beCause my Prophecy will be Fulfilled, and those **"GLORIOUS Swanky Hotels Castles and Fortresses"** will be Built, along with **"The Great World TEMPLE of PEACE!" (The Glory of Jerusalem Arises Again in the Great State of Flexible Texas!) By The Worldwide People's Revolution!®** Book 017B, which will likely have to be Built AFTER the Great Atomic Nightmare, and after the Remaining Americans are taken to Siberian Prison Camps, where they will Discover enough TIME to Study the Inspired Books of the Colorful Peacock from Angel Ridge, which they Refused to Study when they Lived in Peace in **"The Divided States of United Lies!" (The so-called "United States of North America" in Disguise!) By The Worldwide People's Revolution!®** Book 058. Yes, they could have Avoided all such Disasters, just by being Humble and Perfectly HONEST; but, they Like to LIE to themselves and to others. Therefore, they will have to Suffer in some Siberian Prison Camps with Haralan Popov, who was *Tortured for his Faith* in Bulgaria, for 13 Years. [_] Amen! So, let it Be! Amen!

— Chapter 10 —

The Happy Conclusion!

10-01 [_] Now, knowing this, that "All of the Arguments are in Favor of our Selected King, who has Zero Challengers!" (Before you Attend another Election Deception, you should Carefully Study this Inspired Book with an Honest Open Mind!) By The Worldwide People's Revolution!® Book 085, it is Wisest of the Edomites to Avoid any Great Atomic Nightmare, and Demand: "The GREAT Worldwide TELEVISED Court HEARING!" (That Grand Meeting of the Most-Intelligent and Wel-Ejukaatid Miindz!) By The Worldwide People's Revolution!® Book 041C. After all, the Collective Wisdom of ALL of them should easily Defeat "The Swanky Sword of Divine Truths!" (The Most Powerful Weapon in the Whole Universe!) By The Worldwide People's Revolution!® Book 067. But, if not, the Colorful Peacock from Angel Ridge will Help them to Do that: beCause he has no Desire to Witness any Great Atomic Nightmare, nor to Write any Books about it. In Fact, he would much rather Write about the Healthy Happy People who Live within those "GLORIOUS Swanky Hotels Castles and Fortresses!" (Beautiful Planned City States for WISE Intelligent Well-Educated People with Common Sense and Good Understanding!) By The Worldwide People's Revolution!® Book 019B, who are Busy Building their "Beautiful Swanky Stone Dome Home COMPLEXES!" (HOW to Build SECURE Tax-proof, Insurance-proof, Self-air-conditioned, Paint-proof, Rot-proof, Termite-proof, Mouse-proof, Fireproof, Tornado-proof, Hurricane-proof, Thief-proof, and BOMB-PROOF Houses!) By The Worldwide People's Revolution!® Book 102, and Planting their Gardens, according to: "The LUSCIOUS All-Mineral Organic Method of Gardening!" (HOW to Grow DELICIOUS Satisfying Foods for Potential Kingz and Kweenz in Beautiful Swanky PALACES!) By The Worldwide People's Revolution!® Book 021B: beCause, then they will all be Able to Eat at those "Royal Swanky Buffets!" (The Best Feasts in the Whole World!) By The Worldwide People's Revolution!® Book 103, and to Study: "The New MAGNIFIED Version of the Book of ACTS!" (The Understandable Version of the Acts of the Apostles in Plain English!) By The Worldwide People's Revolution!® Book 063, which is a Companion Book of: "The New MAGNIFIED Version of The GOOD NEWS According to Saint LUKE!" (The Magnified Gospel of Saint Luke in Plain English!) By The Worldwide People's Revolution!® Book 061, which is a Companion Book of: "The New MAGNIFIED Version of The GOOD NEWS According to Saint JOHN!" (The Gospel According to Saint John Zebedee Boanerges [pronounced Boo-an-er-jeez] in Plain English!) By The Worldwide People's Revolution!® Book 062, which is a Companion Book of: "The New MAGNIFIED Version of the Book of REVELATION!" (The Understandable Version of the Most-Controversial Book in the Whole World!) By The Worldwide People's Revolution!® Book 105, which is a Companion Book of: "The New MAGNIFIED Version of the Book of DEUTERONOMY!" (The Understandable Version of Deuteronomy in Plain English!) Book 084, which is a Companion Book of: "The New MAGNIFIED Version of the PSALMS of King David!" (The Understandable Version of the Famous Psalms in Plain English!) By The Worldwide People's Revolution!® Book 064, which is a Companion Book of: "Thu Nq MAGNUFIID Verzhun uv Thu PROVERBZ uv KING SOLUMUN in Plaan Ingglish!" (The Understandable Version of the Famous Proverbs of King Solomon in Plain English!) By The Worldwide People's Revolution!® Book 028, which is a Companion Book of: "ECCLESIASTES Uncovered and Recovered!" (The New MAGNIFIED Version of Ecclesiastes and the Song of Solomon in Plain English!) By The Worldwide People's Revolution!® Book 034, which is a Companion Book of: "A Sound Argument for Good Masters and Obedient Servants!" (WHY Everyone Needs a Good Master, and every Master Needs Good Obedient Servants!) By The Worldwide People's Revolution!® Book 008B, which is a Companion Book of: "Has your Life become Extremely Complicated?" (HOW to Live a SIMPLE Life!) By The Worldwide People's Revolution!® Book 068, which is a Companion Book of: "The Swanky Associations of Working Soldiers!" (A Fascinating Collection of Various Kinds of Voluntary Working Soldiers!) By The Worldwide People's Revolution!® Book 018B, which is a Companion Book of: "Seven Great Armies of Working Soldiers!" (HOW to Provide a Way for Everyone to WORK: so as to Eliminate Poverty, Crimes, Drug Abuses, Prisons and Unnecessary Taxes!) By The Worldwide People's Revolution!® Book 015B, which is a Companion Book of: "Poverty Hunger Riots Strikes Police Brutalities Election Deceptions and Civil Wars!" (The High Price that we Earthlings have Paid for Leaving the Good Land!) By The Worldwide People's Revolution!® Book 014B, which is a Companion Book of: "Does a Good Soldier have to be a MURDERER?" (Seven Great Swanky Armies of Voluntary Working Soldiers!) By The Worldwide People's Revolution!® Book 027B, which is a Companion Book of: "God Speaks and the Whole

World Listens!" (Fire on the Mountain from the Burning Bush by the Spirit of Truths!) By The Worldwide People's Revolution!® Book 026B, which is a Companion Book of: "The Seven Basic Spiritual Building Blocks of LIFE!" (Faith Hope Trust Love Patience Persistence and Obedience!) By The Worldwide People's Revolution!® Book 036, which is a Companion Book of: "MARK TWAIN Races for the PRESIDENCY with a Landslide VICTORY!" (The 2020 Presidential Candidates Desperately Need Some STRONG Undefeatable COMPETITION!) By The Worldwide People's Revolution!® Book 033B, which is a Companion Book of: "The CONDENSED Version of MARK TWAIN Races for the PRESIDENCY with a Landslide VICTORY!" (The 2020 Presidential Candidates Desperately Need Some STRONG Undefeatable COMPETITION!) By The Worldwide People's Revolution!® Book 033C, which is a Companion Book of: "The CONSTITUTION for the New RIGHTEOUS One-World Government!" (HOW all Peoples can get True Justice, and Celebrate the Great Year of JUBILEE!) By The Worldwide People's Revolution!® Book 016B, which is a Companion Book of: "101 Good Reasons and Great Advantages for Establishing a Righteous One-World Government!" (Government By the People, Of the People, and For the People!) By The Worldwide People's Revolution!® Book 104, which is a Companion Book of: "Modern Deceived SLAVES!" (10 Simple Steps for Liberating ALL Modern Slaves, Worldwide, Including Yourself!) By Liberty and Justice for ALL! Book 113, which is a Companion Book of: "VOTE for The GOAT!" (The New Political Party that has Guaranteed Solutions for our Massive Problems!) By The Worldwide People's Revolution!® Book 109, which is a Companion Book of: "Our Selected King SPEAKS OUT!" (It is High Time for some Sane Person to get Total Control of this Insane World!) By The Worldwide People's Revolution!® Book 100, which is a Companion Book of: "What is WRong with those Professing Christians?" (A Self-Examination of the Heart of the Body of Good Government!) By The Worldwide People's Revolution!® Book 002, which is a Companion Book of: "Was Billy Graham Greatly Deceived?" (Giving Honor to whom Honor is Due!) By The Worldwide People's Revolution!® Book 083, which is a Companion Book of: "LIGHTNING STRIKES Versus Lightning Bugs!" (HOW you can Become Moderately RICH, without Telling any Lies nor Selling any Trash!) By The Worldwide People's Revolution!® Book 074, which is a Companion Book of: "Are you a Jobless Graduate of the SKQL uv FQLZ?" (HOW to Get a GOUD EJUKAASHUN without Robbing the Bank!) By The Worldwide

People's Revolution!® Book 020B, which is a Companion Book of: "The Public School of IGNERUNT FQLZ!" (HOW we have been GRAATLEE DISEEVD by Capitalism!) By The Worldwide People's Revolution!® Book 024B, which is a Companion Book of: "Why do I have to be Surrounded by CRAZY PEOPLE!" (Do almost all People Feel like they are Surrounded by CRAZY People?) By The Worldwide People's Revolution!® Book 005B, which is a Companion Book of: "The Washington Journal is a FARCE! (C-SPAN Managers are not very WISE!) By The Worldwide People's Revolution!® Book 006C, which is a Companion Book of: "UNLIMITED ENERGY 99 Percent Pollution-Free!" (HOW to Obtain Free ElecTrickery, Worldwide!) By The Worldwide People's Revolution!® Book 029B, which is a Companion Book of: "For the Love of Money!" (The Strange Things that People Say and Do to Get more Money!) By The Worldwide People's Revolution!® Book 003B, which is a Companion Book of: "What is WRong with those CRAZY CHRISTIANS?" (A Self-Examination of the Heart of the Body of Good Government!) By The Worldwide People's Revolution!® Book 076, which is a Companion Book of: "Did God or Satan Ordain Medical Doctors?" (Ask Huck Finn and/or Nigger Jim: because neither Tom Sawyer nor Judge Thatcher would Know!) By The Worldwide People's Revolution!® Book 022B, which is a Companion Book of: "The United States of the Whole World!" (A True Global Economy for the Masses of Working People!) By The Worldwide People's Revolution!® Book 055, which is a Companion Book of: "The Worldwide People's Revolution!" (A Comprehensive Plan for Obtaining Worldwide Law, Order, Obedience, Peace and True Prosperity!) By The Worldwide People's Revolution!® Book 108, which is a Companion Book of: "Should Wives Obey their Husbands?" (OR, Should Husbands OBEY their Wives?) By The Irreverent Penname Mockingbird! Book 112, which is a Companion Book of: "IMPORTANT THINGS that Should Have Been Written in the Holy Bible!" (A Special Challenge to all Professing Christians, Jews, Hindus, Muslims and Atheists!) By The Irreverent Penname Scumbag! Book 110, which is a Companion Book of: "Hosts of HOAXES Live In Under Around and Over the Little White OUTHOUSE!" (WHY Spiritually-Blind Cowardly-Americans are Hunkering Down in their Empty Root Cellars!) By The Irreverent Penname Oversight! Book 111, which is a Companion Book of: "What will you Do when the Rain STOPS?" (God's Last Resort to Save Mankind from his MADNESS!) By The Worldwide People's Revolution!® Book 101.

10-02 [_] So, O Great White Bald Eagle, it appears that the Happy Conclusion is that we Ignorant Fools get to Read no less than 100 Inspired Books, whereby we might keep ourselves Entertained for the next 1,000 Years, or more, by the Colorful Peacock from Angel Ridge. Therefore, this is not such a Sad Story, after all, is it?

10-03 [_] Well, my Friend, that all Depends on how it turns out, in the End.

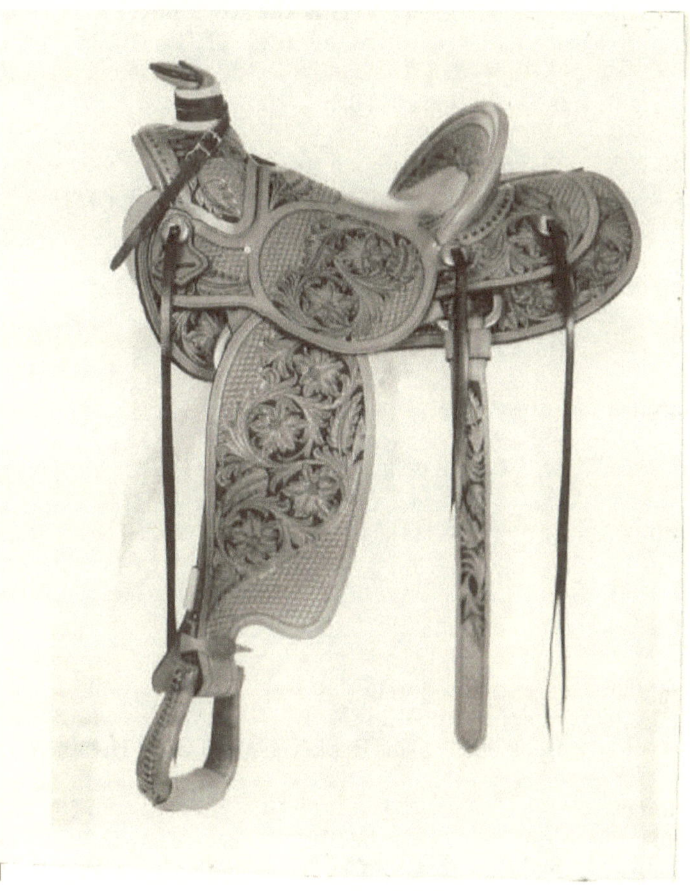

{I am Ready to Ride Off into the Sunset, and Forget it all.}

— Chapter 40 —

A Long List of other Fascinating Literature by the same Inspired Author

[_] 40-001 — "LIGHTNING **Versus the** Lightning Bug!" (HOW almost Everyone can become Moderately RICH, without Telling Any Lies nor Selling Any Capitalist Trash!) By The Worldwide People's Revolution!® Book 001B.

[_] 40-002 — "What is WRong with those Professing Christians?" (A Self-Examination of the Heart of the Body of Good Government!) By The Worldwide People's Revolution!® Book 002.

[_] 40-003 — "For the Love of Money!" (The Strange Things that People Say and Do to Get more Money!) By The Worldwide People's Revolution!® Book 003B.

[_] 40-004 — "How Best to Prepare for CLIMATE CHANGES!" (The Wisest Plan for Mankind to Follow!) By The Worldwide People's Revolution!® Book 004B.

[_] 40-005 — "Why do I have to be Surrounded by CRAZY PEOPLE!" (Do almost all People Feel like they are Surrounded by CRAZY People?) By The Worldwide People's Revolution!® Book 005B.

[_] 40-006 — "The Washington Journal is a FARCE! (C-SPAN Managers are not very WISE!) By The Worldwide People's Revolution!® Book 006C. (This Book has lots of Good Humor.)

[_] 40-007 — "The PRAYERS of PUMPKINHEADS!" (This Book is otherwise known as the Prayers of Preachers, Priests, Professors, Politicians, Prostitutes, Policemen, Pumpkinheads, Punks, Prisoners, and other Professionals — in other Words, the Capital P People!) By The Worldwide People's Revolution!® Book 007B. (Some of it is for Adults only.)

[_] 40-008 — "A Sound Argument for Good Masters and Obedient Servants!" (WHY Everyone Needs a Good Master, and every

Master Needs Good Obedient Servants!) By The Worldwide People's Revolution!® Book 008B.

[_] 40-009 — "WHY are some Preachers so POOR?" (HOW almost all Preachers can Get Moderately RICH, without Preaching any Outlandish LIES!) By The Worldwide People's Revolution!® Book 009B.

[_] 40-010 — "GOOD NEWS for REBEL WOMEN!" (HOW almost all Wives can become Moderately RICH without Leaving their Homes! Guaranteed!) By The Worldwide People's Revolution!® Book 010B.

[_] 40-011 — "The Low Court of Supreme Injustices is Brought to Trial!" (Our Selected King Butts Heads with the United States Supreme Court, with or without their Black Robes of Hypocrisies and Lies!) By The Worldwide People's Revolution!® Book 011B. (This Inspired Book contains the Famous *Declaration of Interdependence,* which is a Must Read. It also contains the Correct Wording for the Placard on the Statue of Liberty.)

[_] 40-012 — "The Right Design for Living!" (A List of Great Advantages for Building Beautiful Planned City States!) By The Worldwide People's Revolution!® Book 012B. (This Book contains many Important Drawings, as well as HOW to Save hundreds of Trillions of Dollars by Building Swanky Fortresses, and Living in Peace within them. It is a Companion Book of Book 011B, which contains many more Great Advantages for Swanky Fortresses.)

[_] 40-013 — **"The Gospel According to The Worldwide People's Revolution!®" (The Good News from the Most Modern Perspective!)** See Book 077. (This Book contains the Famous Sermon of Jonah to the Ninevites, whereby 120,000 People Repented in Sackcloth and Ashes! Do not Miss Out on it. Not even the Rev. Dr. Billy Graham got 120,000 Converts during one Day!)

[_] 40-014 — **"Poverty Hunger Riots Strikes Police Brutalities Election Deceptions and Civil Wars!" (The High Price that we Earthlings have Paid for Leaving the Good Land!) By The Worldwide People's Revolution!® Book 014B.**

[_] 40-015 — **"Seven Great Armies of Working Soldiers!" (HOW to Provide a Way for Everyone to WORK: so as to Eliminate Poverty,**

Crimes, Drug Abuses, Prisons and Unnecessary Taxes!) By The Worldwide People's Revolution!® Book 015B. (This Book contains a True-Life Story when the Author was in the Army.)

[_] 40-016 — "The CONSTITUTION for the New RIGHTEOUS One-World Government!" (HOW all Peoples can get True Justice, and Celebrate the Great Year of JUBILEE!) By The Worldwide People's Revolution!® Book 016B.

[_] 40-017 — "The Great World TEMPLE of PEACE!" (The Glory of Jerusalem Arises Again in the Great State of Flexible Texas!) By The Worldwide People's Revolution!® Book 017B.

[_] 40-018 — "The Swanky Associations of Working Soldiers!" (A Fascinating Collection of Various Kinds of Voluntary Working Soldiers!) By The Worldwide People's Revolution!® Book 018B. (There will be thousands of Associations for all Kinds of Occupations, which will Specialize in Fine Arts — such as Hand-carved Leather-bound Books. See "LIGHTNING STRIKES Versus Lightning Bugs!" (HOW you can Become Moderately RICH, without Telling any Lies nor Selling any Trash!) By The Worldwide People's Revolution!® Book 074, for a Picture of a Good Example.)

[_] 40-019 — "GLORIOUS Swanky Hotels Castles and Fortresses!" (Beautiful Planned City States for WISE Intelligent Well-Educated People with Common Sense and Good Understanding!) By The Worldwide People's Revolution!® Book 019B. (This Book contains many Rough Drawings, which could be Greatly Improved upon by someone who Knows the Art, and has the Correct Computer Programs for doing it.)

[_] 40-020 — "Are you a Jobless Graduate of the SKQL uv FQLZ?" (HOW to Get a GOUD EJUKAASHUN without Robbing the Bank!) By The Worldwide People's Revolution!® Book 020B. (This Inspired Book contains the New MAGNIFIED Version {NMV} of *First Corinthians 13,* plus: HOW to Produce Pure Living Water!)

[_] 40-021 — "The LUSCIOUS All-Mineral Organic Method of Gardening!" (HOW to Grow DELICIOUS Satisfying Foods for Potential Kingz and Kweenz in Beautiful Swanky PALACES!) By The Worldwide People's Revolution!® Book 021B. (This Book Explains HOW to make a Flood-proof Garden, while Trapping the Rainwater.)

[_] 40-022 — "Did God or Satan Ordain Medical Doctors?" (Ask Huck Finn and/or Nigger Jim: because neither Tom Sawyer nor Judge Thatcher would Know!) By The Worldwide People's Revolution!® Book 022B. (This Inspired Book Reveals HOW to Prevent Common Colds, and has a Special Chapter that Explains what a True "Nigger" IS. Surprise yourself!)

[_] 40-023 — "The BIG White OUTHOUSE on the Not-so-Biblical Capitol DUNGHILL!" (The Chief Sins of the Divided States of United Lies!) By The Worldwide People's Revolution!® Book 023B. (This Book contains Special Words that most People have never Heard! Surprise yourself again!)

[_] 40-024 — "The Public School of IGNERUNT FQLZ!" (HOW we have been GRAATLEE DISEEVD by Capitalism!) By The Worldwide People's Revolution!® Book 024B. (This Book Teaches Children HOW to "Reed and Riit in Funetik Ingglish in just wun Daa!" You should Challenge your Frendz and Naaberz with it.)

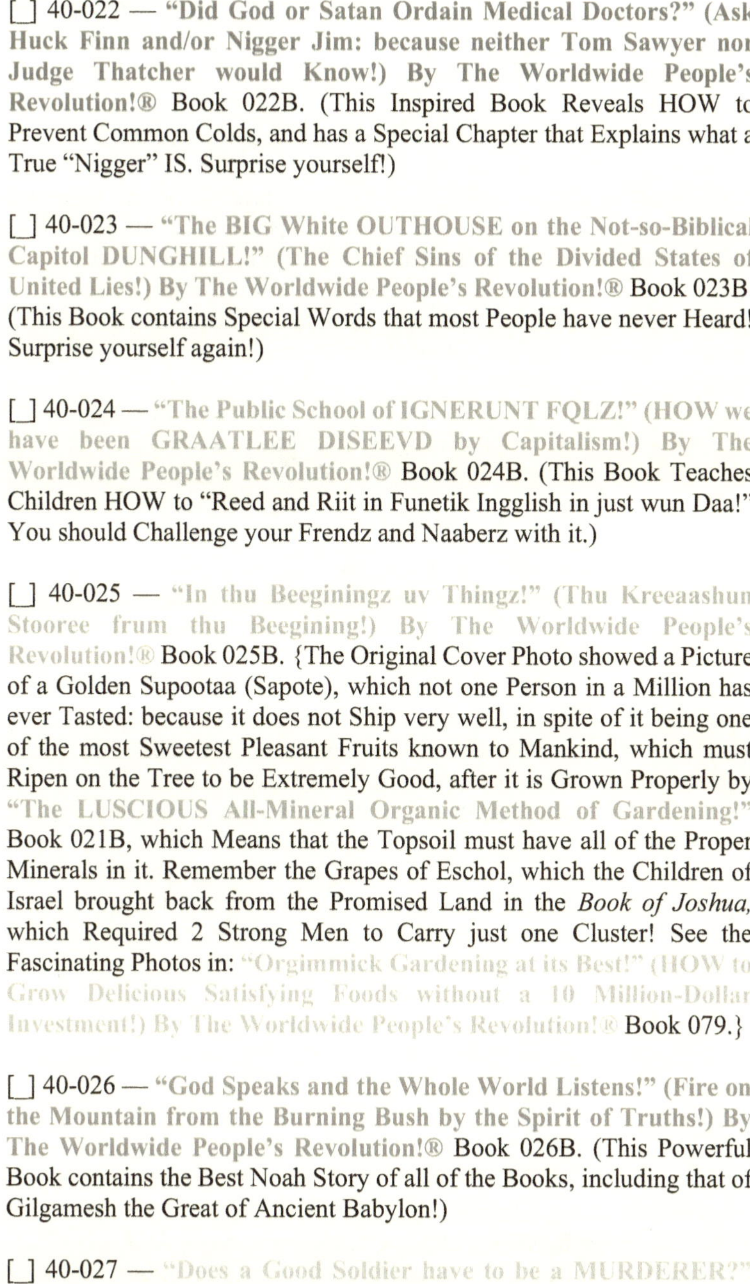

[_] 40-025 — "In thu Beeginingz uv Thingz!" (Thu Kreeaashun Stooree frum thu Beegining!) By The Worldwide People's Revolution!® Book 025B. {The Original Cover Photo showed a Picture of a Golden Supootaa (Sapote), which not one Person in a Million has ever Tasted: because it does not Ship very well, in spite of it being one of the most Sweetest Pleasant Fruits known to Mankind, which must Ripen on the Tree to be Extremely Good, after it is Grown Properly by "The LUSCIOUS All-Mineral Organic Method of Gardening!" Book 021B, which Means that the Topsoil must have all of the Proper Minerals in it. Remember the Grapes of Eschol, which the Children of Israel brought back from the Promised Land in the *Book of Joshua,* which Required 2 Strong Men to Carry just one Cluster! See the Fascinating Photos in: "Orgimmick Gardening at its Best!" (HOW to Grow Delicious Satisfying Foods without a 10 Million-Dollar Investment!) By The Worldwide People's Revolution!® Book 079.}

[_] 40-026 — "God Speaks and the Whole World Listens!" (Fire on the Mountain from the Burning Bush by the Spirit of Truths!) By The Worldwide People's Revolution!® Book 026B. (This Powerful Book contains the Best Noah Story of all of the Books, including that of Gilgamesh the Great of Ancient Babylon!)

[_] 40-027 — "Does a Good Soldier have to be a MURDERER?" (Seven Great Swanky Armies of Voluntary Working Soldiers!) By

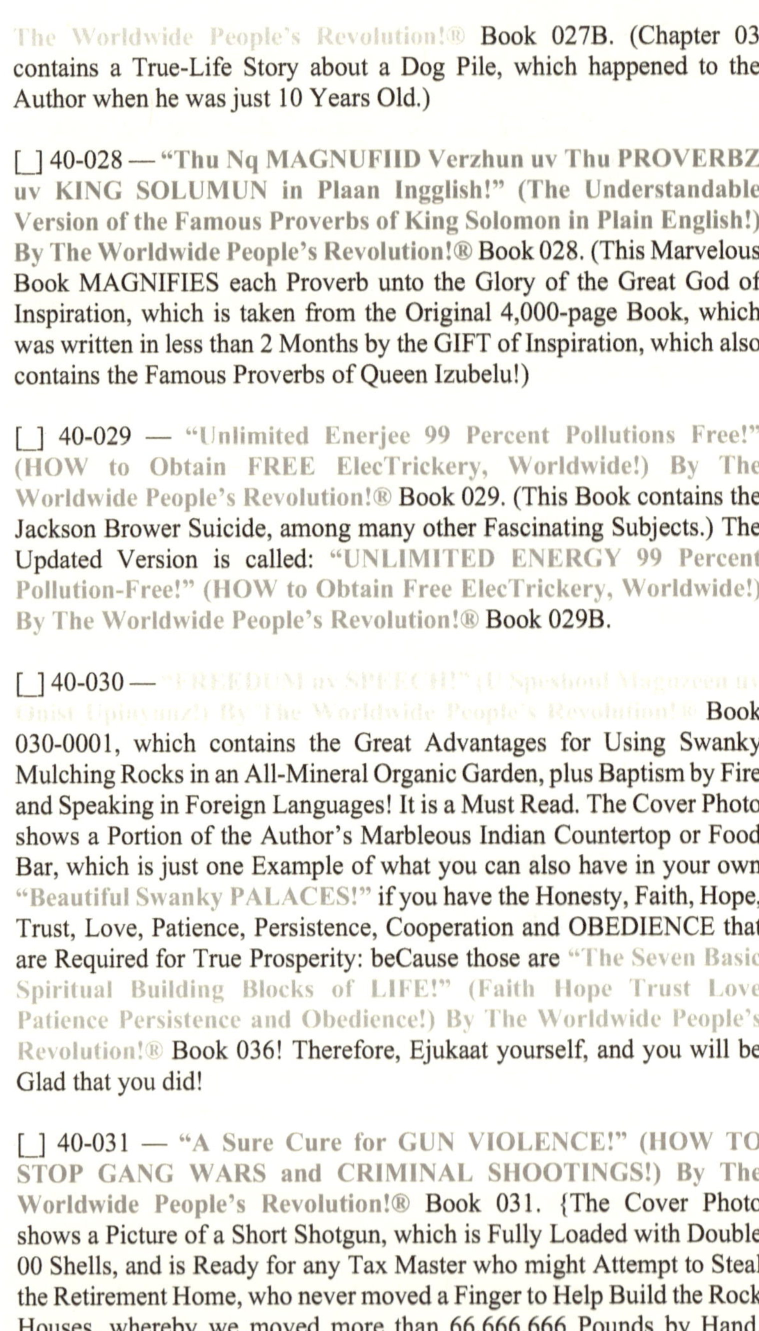

The Worldwide People's Revolution!® Book 027B. (Chapter 03 contains a True-Life Story about a Dog Pile, which happened to the Author when he was just 10 Years Old.)

[_] 40-028 — "Thu Nq MAGNUFIID Verzhun uv Thu PROVERBZ uv KING SOLUMUN in Plaan Ingglish!" (The Understandable Version of the Famous Proverbs of King Solomon in Plain English!) By The Worldwide People's Revolution!® Book 028. (This Marvelous Book MAGNIFIES each Proverb unto the Glory of the Great God of Inspiration, which is taken from the Original 4,000-page Book, which was written in less than 2 Months by the GIFT of Inspiration, which also contains the Famous Proverbs of Queen Izubelu!)

[_] 40-029 — "Unlimited Enerjee 99 Percent Pollutions Free!" (HOW to Obtain FREE ElecTrickery, Worldwide!) By The Worldwide People's Revolution!® Book 029. (This Book contains the Jackson Brower Suicide, among many other Fascinating Subjects.) The Updated Version is called: "UNLIMITED ENERGY 99 Percent Pollution-Free!" (HOW to Obtain Free ElecTrickery, Worldwide!) By The Worldwide People's Revolution!® Book 029B.

[_] 40-030 — "FREEDUM uv SPEECH!" (Uu Speshuul Magazeen uv Onist Upinyunz!) By The Worldwide People's Revolution!® Book 030-0001, which contains the Great Advantages for Using Swanky Mulching Rocks in an All-Mineral Organic Garden, plus Baptism by Fire and Speaking in Foreign Languages! It is a Must Read. The Cover Photo shows a Portion of the Author's Marbleous Indian Countertop or Food Bar, which is just one Example of what you can also have in your own "Beautiful Swanky PALACES!" if you have the Honesty, Faith, Hope, Trust, Love, Patience, Persistence, Cooperation and OBEDIENCE that are Required for True Prosperity: beCause those are "The Seven Basic Spiritual Building Blocks of LIFE!" (Faith Hope Trust Love Patience Persistence and Obedience!) By The Worldwide People's Revolution!® Book 036! Therefore, Ejukaat yourself, and you will be Glad that you did!

[_] 40-031 — "A Sure Cure for GUN VIOLENCE!" (HOW TO STOP GANG WARS and CRIMINAL SHOOTINGS!) By The Worldwide People's Revolution!® Book 031. {The Cover Photo shows a Picture of a Short Shotgun, which is Fully Loaded with Double 00 Shells, and is Ready for any Tax Master who might Attempt to Steal the Retirement Home, who never moved a Finger to Help Build the Rock Houses, whereby we moved more than 66,666,666 Pounds by Hand, whose Property was Cunningly Stolen by that False Anti-Christ WICKED Cover-up Government, which allowed Bankers to Rob us of 30 Years of Hard Labor and more than 300,000 dollars-worth of Investments in our Uncommon American Farm, which is Explained in: "LIGHTNING STRIKES Versus Lightning Bugs!" (HOW you can Become Moderately RICH, without Telling any Lies nor Selling any Trash!) By The Worldwide People's Revolution!® Book 074, which contains many Photographs with Profound Explanations! Do not be left out in the Darkness of Ignorance. Get Informed, now: beCause, **"The Great False Economy is now DEBUNKED!"** Book 053.}

[_] 40-032 — "AIIRMWVC and Reasonable Solutions!" (Aliens, Illegal Immigrants, Refugees, Migrant Workers and other Victims of Capitalism!) By The Worldwide People's Revolution!® Book 032. (This Inspired Book contains *the New MAGNIFIED Version of Job 33*.)

[_] 40-033 — "MARK TWAIN Races for the PRESIDENCY with a Landslide VICTORY!" (The 2020 Presidential Candidates Desperately Need Some STRONG Undefeatable COMPETITION!) By The Worldwide People's Revolution!® Book 033B. {This Book contains a Part of the Author's Autobiography, and his Personal Answers to the Questions in: "The Complete SURVEYS of our VALUES!" (SURVEYS of Religious Spiritual Political Governmental Sexual Social Moral Economic Business Labor Habitual and Miscellaneous VALUES!) Book 059. **The CONDENSED Version** is Book 033C, which most People Prefer.}

[_] 40-034 — "ECCLESIASTES Uncovered and Recovered!" (The New MAGNIFIED Version of Ecclesiastes and the Song of Solomon in Plain English!) By The Worldwide People's Revolution!® Book 034. (This is the Book that contains the Famous Sayings for *There is a Time to be Born, and a Time to Die ..."* which has been Greatly Magnified!)

[_] 40-035 — "The Environmentalists' Perfect Paradise!" (HOW almost Everyone can be Living in a Beautiful Manmade Paradise!) By The Worldwide People's Revolution!® Book 035C. (This Book contains the NMV of *Psalm 48,* which will Amaze you, O Lady Doubtfulness!)

[_] 40-036 — "The Seven Basic Spiritual Building Blocks of LIFE!" (Faith Hope Trust Love Patience Persistence and Obedience!) By The Worldwide People's Revolution!® Book 036. (This Book contains the Mockingbird's Version of *Hebrews 11,* plus the NMV of *First Corinthians 13,* among many other "Goodies.")

[ ] 40-037 — "DIETS!" (A Reasonable Solution for the "Eternal Controversy"!) By The Worldwide People's Revolution!® Book 037.

[ ] 40-038 — "The Nature of CAPITALISM!" (A List of the EVILS of CAPITALISM!) By The Worldwide People's Revolution!® Book 038.

[ ] 40-039 — "SWANGKEENOMIKS Rules the Roost!" (HOW all People can Prosper in a RIIT WAA, and STOP Polluting the Earth with Capitalist TRASH!) By The Worldwide People's Revolution!® Book 039. (The Cover Photo shows a Portion of the Author's Retirement Home, before the 5,000+ square-feet Concrete Roof was Installed, after moving more than 66 Million Pounds by Hand, and mostly by his own Boastful Hands!)

[ ] 40-040 — "The New MAGNIFIED Version of The Book of MORMON!" (The Story of the White and Dark Indians in the Americas!) By The Worldwide People's Revolution!® Book 040, which comes in 2 Volumes of about 500 Pages, each. The Cover Photo on the First Volume shows the Queen of England's Golden Coach, and the Cover Photo on the Second Volume shows one of many Polished Spanish Marble Walls in our Selected King's Retirement Home, which is worth a thousand dollars per square yard, which is another Example of what you can also have, if you simply OBEY your Righteous KING! All such Marble is very Inspiring. No one could Study it for very long without Believing in a Great Creator God. The Picture does not do it Justice. You would have to See it in Person, and Wash it with Pure Water to bring Out the Beauty of it.

[ ] 40-041 — "The GREAT Worldwide TELEVISED Court HEARING!" (That Grand Meeting of the Most-Intelligent and Wel-Ejukaatid Miindz!) By The Worldwide People's Revolution!® Book 041C. {This is the Book that the World has long been Waiting for: beCause it will Overthrow the Evil Empires, and make it Possible to Establish "The New RIGHTEOUS One-World Government!" (HOW to Establish a Righteous One-World Government without Going to WAR!) By The Worldwide People's Revolution!® Book 056. This is the Greatest Idea since the Invention of the Light Bulb, Guaranteed!}

[_] 40-042 — "The Secret City of the Great King!" (HOW the True Church will Escape from the Great Tribulation!) By The Worldwide People's Revolution!® Book 042. (Be Sure to Inform your Friends, Relatives and Naaberz about this Wonderful Book: beCause they might also Want to Escape!)

[_] 40-043 — "Terrorists Beware that your Days are Numbered!" (HOW to Bring those Terrorist Attacks to a Screeching HALT!) By The Worldwide People's Revolution!® Book 043. (This Book also contains the Fascinating Book of LEHI, which has now been Restored!) †‡

[_] 40-044 — "The New MAGNIFIED Version of ISAIAH in Plain English!" (The Understandable Version of the Book of Isaiah!) By The Worldwide People's Revolution!® Book 044. (The Cover Photo shows a Swanky Potato and Avocado Salad with Sweet Peas and Corn, among other "Secret" Ingredients, which are Revealed within the Book. Remember that you can read many Words for Free in the Book Previews on www.Amazon.com.usa or UK.)

[_] 40-045 — "HOW to Become a HOLY Man!" (40 Good Reasons WHY People Should FAST and PRAY!) By The Worldwide People's Revolution!® Book 045, which is a Companion Book of:

[_] 40-046 — "The Proper RULES for FASTING!" (The Complete Instruction Manual for True Repentance!) By The Worldwide People's Revolution!® Book 046, which is a Companion Book of the above-mentioned Book, which contains a True-Life Story about an Old Black Mare called Lucy, who Fasted for 30 Days without Food nor Water, who was Physiologically "Born Again," as Jesus might say. See the Full Details in: "The New MAGNIFIED Version of The GOOD NEWS According to Saint JOHN!" (The Gospel According to Saint John Zebedee Boanerges in Plain English!) Book 062, which contains many Inspiring Photographs with Explanations!

[_] 40-047 — "Are Americans the Most-STUPID People who ever Lived?" (HOW Working People can PROSPER and Live in PEACE Under the Rulership of a RIGHTEOUS KING!) By The Worldwide People's Revolution!® Book 047. (The Cover Photo shows a large Portion of the Author's Living Room Floor, which is worth 100,000$, which is just another Good Example of what you can also have, just for Loving and Obeying your Elected King!)

[_] 40-048 — "An Amazing Collection of Wit and Wisdom!" (The Marvelous Tale of the Colorful Peacock from Angel Ridge, and the Strong Rope of Everlasting Hope!) By The Worldwide People's Revolution!® Book 048. (The Cover Photo shows a Book Display, which will be Greatly Enhanced during the Future, when all 364+ Inspired Books are on Display in a Swanky Truth-brary, as Opposed to the Public LIE-brary.)

[_] 40-049 — "Justifications for Capitalizations!" (WHY our Selected King DEFIES the School of FOOLS by Capitalizing LOVE and HATE!) By The Worldwide People's Revolution!® Book 049.

[_] 40-050 — "The END of CONFUSION!" (The Great CELEBRATION of the Magnificent Wedding of the Most-Humble, Honest Nations, and the Grand Year of JUBILEE!) By The Worldwide People's Revolution!® Book 050. (Just Try to Visualize those **"Seven Great Swanky Armies of Voluntary Working Soldiers"** Marching through the Valley of Megiddo, being Dressed in their Colorful Robes, while the Band Plays *The Battle Hymn of the Republic,* and the Choirs Sing the Praises of the Great KING of Kings! What a Sight and Sound that will be, which will be Climaxed in "The Great World TEMPLE of PEACE," when the Nations will get Married, along with our Elected King! Come one, come all to "The GREAT Worldwide TELEVISED Court HEARING," by Means of your Wide Flat-screen TVs, whereby you might Learn WHY, WHEN and HOW!) †‡

[_] 40-051 — "The Loathsome Burdens of the Independent Jackasses!" (A New Civilized Approach for Quietly Solving our Massive Problems!) By The Worldwide People's Revolution!® Book 051. (Just Think about the Multitude of almost Worthless Meetings of the Minds, who Strained themselves to Think of Reasonable Solutions for our Massive Problems, who sometimes even Prayed to God for Help; but, the Best Solutions have been here for no less than 40 Years — Thanks to the Spirit of Inspiration from GOD!)

[_] 40-052 — "Are we Tax Slaves of a Lower Order than those Lying Conniving EDOMITES!" (HOW to be Liberated From all Forms of Slavery, Worldwide!) By The Worldwide People's Revolution!® Book 052B. {This Inspired Book once had another Title and Author, which was not Acceptable by Amazon, which has now been Restored in all of its Glory, and is Published by more Trustworthy People, who are not Afraid of Controversies, nor of: "The Swanky Sword of Divine

Truths!" (The Most-Powerful Weapon in the Whole Universe!) By The Worldwide People's Revolution!® Book 067.}

[ ] 40-053 — "The Great False Economy is now DEBUNKED!" (Adolf Hitler had a much Better Economic System!) By The Worldwide People's Revolution!® Book 053. {Trust me, Adolf was no Saint; but, during the Day of God's Judgment, he will be Justified, while his Anti-Christ Opponents will be Condemned: beCause they Refused to Attend a Worldwide Radio Debate with Adolf Hitler, whose Arguments will Stand Up during the Day of Judgment, which would have Prevented World War 2, and thus Saved the Lives of no less than 60 Million People! Likewise, we Tax Slaves must now Act more Wisely, and DEMAND "The GREAT Worldwide TELEVISED Court HEARING," Book 041B, whereby we might Save the World from that Dreadful Battle of Megiddo, called *Armageddon!* Yes, the Ball is now in YOUR Hands, O Potential Friend or Enemy, and you are now Responsible for it. Therefore, do not Shirk your Duty as a Free Citizen; but, Help us to Spread this Message, far and wide, whereby the Masses of People will be Demanding The GWTCH, and thus, Prevent "The Great ATOMIC NIGHTMARE!" (The Saddest Story in World History!) By The Great White Bald Eagle! Book 099.}

[ ] 40-054 — "The UGLY Scarred Dishonest Face of Poor Old Miserable UNCLE SAM!" (A Memorial Day Legacy!) By The Worldwide People's Revolution!® Book 054. {NOTE: This Inspired Book was also Suppressed by Amazon, who will be most Ashamed of themselves if they do not Un-suppress it during the Future: beCause it will also be Published by People of Greater Faith, who Know for a Fact that it is the TRUTH! Therefore, just be Patient. Search for Book 054B, *King James Version.*}

[ ] 40-055 — "The United States of the Whole World!" (A True Global Economy for the Masses of Working People!) By The Worldwide People's Revolution!® Book 055. (This Inspired Book contains many Colored Photographs with Explanations. It is a Good Book to Publish in Foreign Nations, who are not so Blinded by their Pride, who can See the Mountain of Lies much Better at a Distance from them: beCause of not being a Part of the American Corruption.) †‡

[ ] 40-056 — "The New RIGHTEOUS One-World Government!" (HOW to Establish a Righteous One-World Government without Going to WAR!) By The Worldwide People's Revolution!® Book

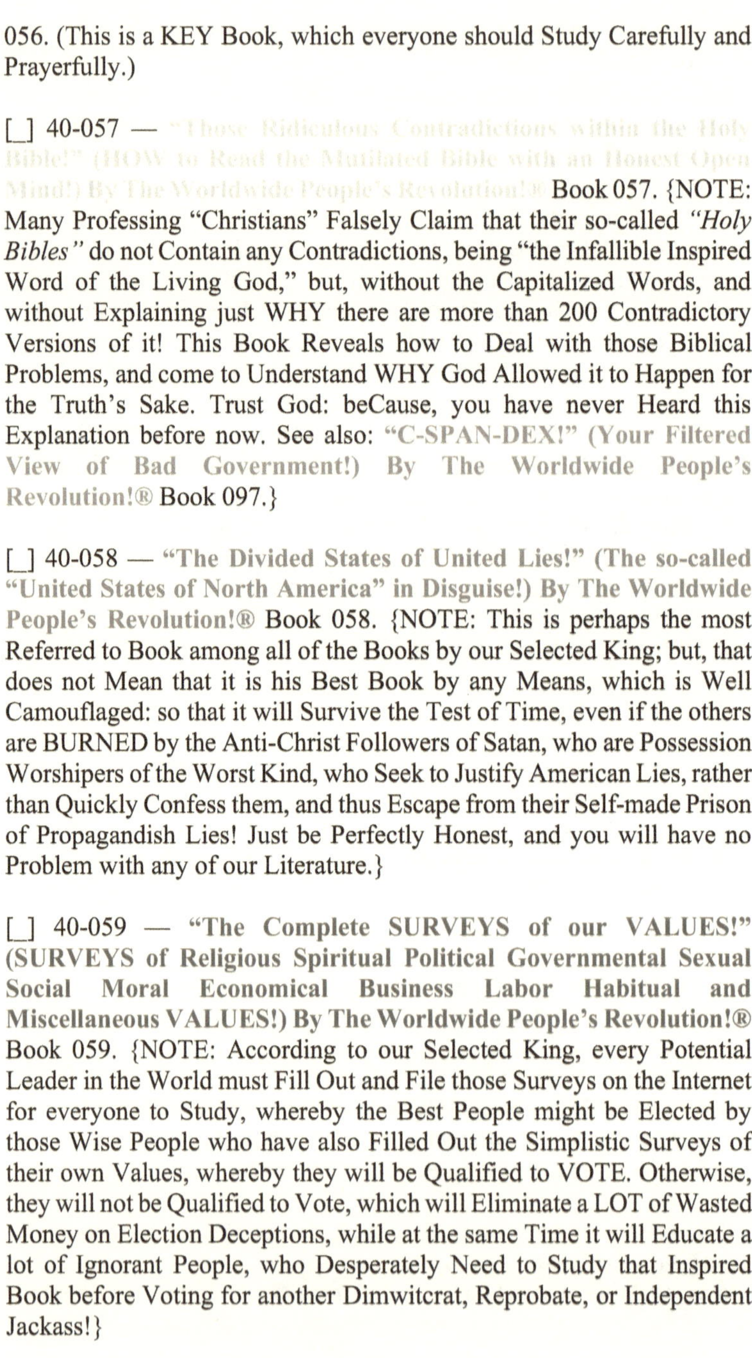

056. (This is a KEY Book, which everyone should Study Carefully and Prayerfully.)

[_] 40-057 — "Those Ridiculous Contradictions within the Holy Bible!" (HOW to Read the Mutilated Bible with an Honest Open Mind!) By The Worldwide People's Revolution!® Book 057. {NOTE: Many Professing "Christians" Falsely Claim that their so-called "Holy Bibles" do not Contain any Contradictions, being "the Infallible Inspired Word of the Living God," but, without the Capitalized Words, and without Explaining just WHY there are more than 200 Contradictory Versions of it! This Book Reveals how to Deal with those Biblical Problems, and come to Understand WHY God Allowed it to Happen for the Truth's Sake. Trust God: beCause, you have never Heard this Explanation before now. See also: "C-SPAN-DEX!" (Your Filtered View of Bad Government!) By The Worldwide People's Revolution!® Book 097.}

[_] 40-058 — "The Divided States of United Lies!" (The so-called "United States of North America" in Disguise!) By The Worldwide People's Revolution!® Book 058. {NOTE: This is perhaps the most Referred to Book among all of the Books by our Selected King; but, that does not Mean that it is his Best Book by any Means, which is Well Camouflaged: so that it will Survive the Test of Time, even if the others are BURNED by the Anti-Christ Followers of Satan, who are Possession Worshipers of the Worst Kind, who Seek to Justify American Lies, rather than Quickly Confess them, and thus Escape from their Self-made Prison of Propagandish Lies! Just be Perfectly Honest, and you will have no Problem with any of our Literature.}

[_] 40-059 — "The Complete SURVEYS of our VALUES!" (SURVEYS of Religious Spiritual Political Governmental Sexual Social Moral Economical Business Labor Habitual and Miscellaneous VALUES!) By The Worldwide People's Revolution!® Book 059. {NOTE: According to our Selected King, every Potential Leader in the World must Fill Out and File those Surveys on the Internet for everyone to Study, whereby the Best People might be Elected by those Wise People who have also Filled Out the Simplistic Surveys of their own Values, whereby they will be Qualified to VOTE. Otherwise, they will not be Qualified to Vote, which will Eliminate a LOT of Wasted Money on Election Deceptions, while at the same Time it will Educate a lot of Ignorant People, who Desperately Need to Study that Inspired Book before Voting for another Dimwitcrat, Reprobate, or Independent Jackass!}

[_] 40-059B — **"The Simplistic SURVEYS of our VALUES!"** Book 059B. (The Cover Photo shows some Beautiful African Antelopes, who are Free with a Capital F.)

[_] 40-060 — "HOW to Get our PRIORITIES in ORDER!" (The Glories of Democracy; and, Does DEMON-ocracy have its Priorities in Order?) By The Worldwide People's Revolution!® Book 060. This Book will need to be Re-written by a Collective Group of Wise People, who will Contribute their True-Life Stories during the Future, when they Wake Up and come to their Right Senses with the Prodigal Son of *Luke 15*. See:

[_] 40-061 — "The New MAGNIFIED Version of The GOOD NEWS According to Saint LUKE!" (The Magnified Gospel of Saint Luke in Plain English!) By The Worldwide People's Revolution!® Book 061, which is by Far the Best Version of that Gospel on the Earth, which has no Rivals at all among the other 200+ Versions. Guaranteed!

[_] 40-062 — "The New MAGNIFIED Version of The GOOD NEWS According to Saint JOHN!" (The Gospel According to Saint John Zebedee Boanerges [pronounced Boo-an-er-jeez] in Plain English!) By The Worldwide People's Revolution!® Book 062, which also has no Rivals among all of the other Versions: beCause this is no Translation of anything; but, it is the Inspired Words of the Living God, which were Revealed by the Holy Spirit to our Selected King, who has not Died, yet.

[_] 40-063 — "The New MAGNIFIED Version of the Book of ACTS!" (The Understandable Version of the Acts of the Apostles in Plain English!) By The Worldwide People's Revolution!® Book 063. (This Inspired Book makes it Understandable WHY the Jews Hated the Apostles so much. You will have to Read it to Believe it.)

[_] 40-064 — "The New MAGNIFIED Version of the PSALMS of King David!" (The Understandable Version of the Famous Psalms in Plain English!) By The Worldwide People's Revolution!® Book 064. You will be Amazed!

[_] 40-065 — "A List of FAIR Swanky Wages!" (The Equitable Wage System!) By The Worldwide People's Revolution!® Book 065. (All Hardworking People will LOVE this Good Book! You will also, if you Study it Carefully.)

[ ] 40-066 — "Beautiful Swanky PALACES!" (A New Concept in Living Habits — Swanky Palaces for Poor People!) By The Worldwide People's Revolution!® Book 066. (You have no Idea what a "Swanky Palace" IS, unless you have read this Unique Book, or another one that Describes those Palaces, and several of them do; but, this one has the Best Description. ENJOY!)

[ ] 40-067 — "The Swanky Sword of Divine Truths!" (The Most Powerful Weapon in the Whole Universe!) By The Worldwide People's Revolution!® Book 067. (The very Reason that our Selected King has no Rivals is beCause of the Swanky Sword of Divine Truths, which no one can Defeat by any Means. Therefore, you Need to have it on your own Side, whereby no one can Defeat your Arguments! Be Strong, be Brave, have Faith and put on the Whole Armor of GOD!)

[ ] 40-068 — "Has your Life become Extremely Complicated?" (HOW to Live a SIMPLE Life!) By The Worldwide People's Revolution!® Book 068. (Many People are not even Aware of just how Complicated their Lives are, until suddenly they are ready to Commit Suicide! It is Best to Prevent all such Evil Things, and this Book tells HOW.)

[ ] 40-069 — "The IDEAL Place to Live!" (HOW to Discover the Ideal Place to Live!) By The Worldwide People's Revolution!® Book 069. {NOTE: Our Selected King Searched the World over, and did not Discover any Idea Place to Live. Therefore, he Concluded that we must Make our own. Yes, we must Build those "GLORIOUS Swanky Hotels Castles and Fortresses!" (Beautiful Planned City States for WISE Intelligent Well-Educated People with Common Sense and Good Understanding!) By The Worldwide People's Revolution!® Book 019B, even if we must DRAFT "Seven Great Armies of Working Soldiers!" (HOW to Provide a Way for Everyone to WORK: so as to Eliminate Poverty, Crimes, Drug Abuses, Prisons and Unnecessary Taxes!) By The Worldwide People's Revolution!® Book 015B; and what on this Good Earth could Prove to be more Profitable than that, and without going to WAR?}

[ ] 40-070 — "Our Elected King Who Speaks Out!" (It is High Time for some Sane Person to Get Control of this Insane World!) By The Worldwide People's Revolution!® Book 070. (This Inspired Book contains a Special Speech that is Addressed to both Houses of the Congress in Washington. You will Love it, O Honest Man of Greater Faith!)

[_] 40-071 — "How GAY is GOD?" (Oh, the Wonders of it all, when it ALL Hangs Out!) By The Worldwide People's Revolution!® Book 071. (Do not Judge the Book, until you have Carefully "Red" all of it. You will be Surprised by the Provable Truths within it, and Greatly Humored by the Author's Exceptionally Good Humor, who is less Gay than God, who has never had any Sexual Intercourse during his entire Life! In other Words, he is a VIRGIN!)

[_] 40-072 — "LIGHTNING STRIKES Versus Lightning Bugs and Impotent Fireflies!" (A Memorial Photo Album of some Real American Heroes!) By The Worldwide People's Revolution!® Book 072. (NOTE: This Book is Unique among all of the Books by our Selected King: beCause he did not get to Proof-read it before the Computer Crashed. It just Happened to be Saved on a Computer Chip before the Computer Crashed, and therefore it was Saved in PDF. But, the Corrections did not get made, which makes it a Special Collector's Item, which has more than 100 Colored Photos, which was what Caused the Crash.) †‡

[_] 40-073 — "The BEST of CAPITALISM!" (Corrections for: "LIGHTNING STRIKES Versus Lightning Bugs and Impotent Fireflies!") Book 073. (It is a completely new Book, except for those Corrections; and it is one of the Best Books in the World, which all Honest People will Love.)

[_] 40-074 — "LIGHTNING STRIKES Versus Lightning Bugs!" (HOW you can Become Moderately RICH, without Telling any Lies nor Selling any Trash!) By The Worldwide People's Revolution!® Book 074, which is the Perfection of all of the Lightning Striking Books, which is Recommended above all others for Mass Production: beCause it stands the Best Chance of being a Real Winner, just after this Book that you are now Reading, which has a Magnetizing Title!

[_] 40-075 — **"What are the Punishments for Dietary Sins?" (Have we Served ourselves Well at the Tables of our Lusts?)** Book 075. (This Book is too Controversial to be Published at this Time. Be very Patient until it is Available: beCause it is HOT!)

[_] 40-076 — "What is WRong with those CRAZY CHRISTIANS?" (A Self-Examination of the Heart of the Body of Good Government!) By The Worldwide People's Revolution!® Book 076.

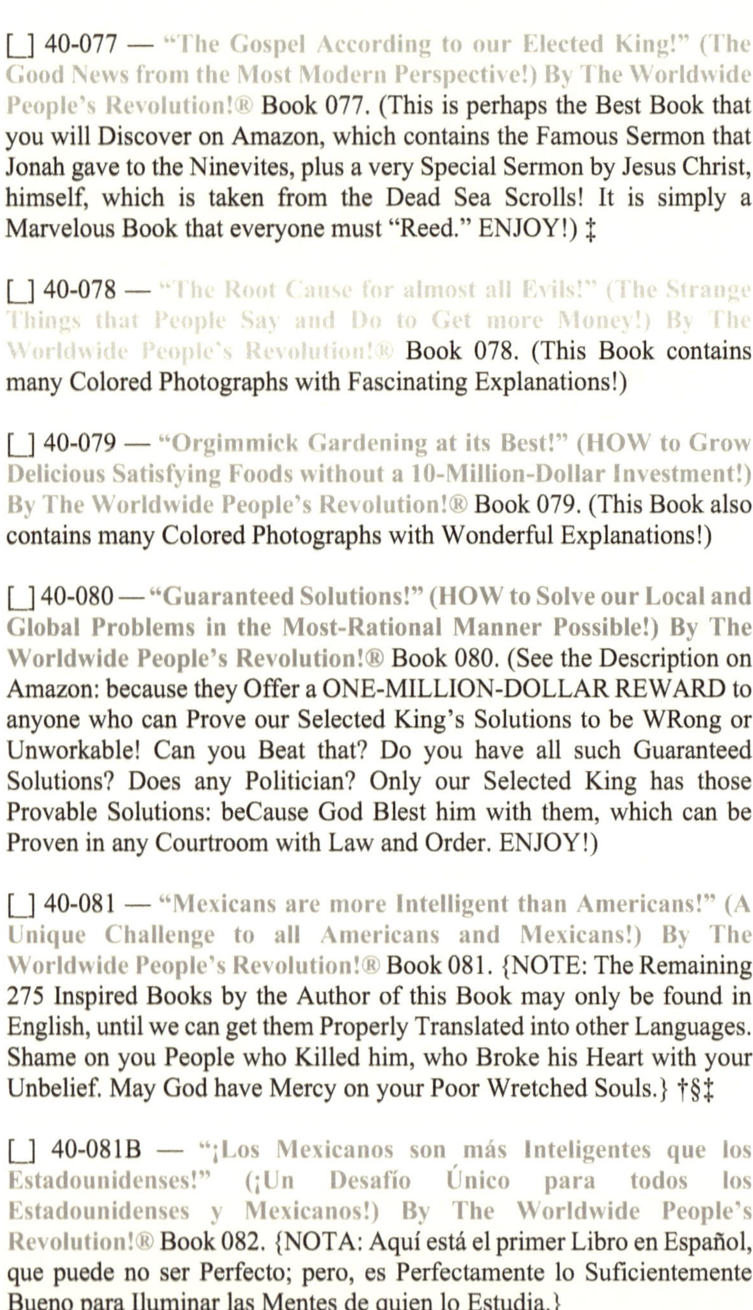

[_] 40-077 — "The Gospel According to our Elected King!" (The Good News from the Most Modern Perspective!) By The Worldwide People's Revolution!® Book 077. (This is perhaps the Best Book that you will Discover on Amazon, which contains the Famous Sermon that Jonah gave to the Ninevites, plus a very Special Sermon by Jesus Christ, himself, which is taken from the Dead Sea Scrolls! It is simply a Marvelous Book that everyone must "Reed." ENJOY!) ‡

[_] 40-078 — "The Root Cause for almost all Evils!" (The Strange Things that People Say and Do to Get more Money!) By The Worldwide People's Revolution!® Book 078. (This Book contains many Colored Photographs with Fascinating Explanations!)

[_] 40-079 — "Orgimmick Gardening at its Best!" (HOW to Grow Delicious Satisfying Foods without a 10-Million-Dollar Investment!) By The Worldwide People's Revolution!® Book 079. (This Book also contains many Colored Photographs with Wonderful Explanations!)

[_] 40-080 — "Guaranteed Solutions!" (HOW to Solve our Local and Global Problems in the Most-Rational Manner Possible!) By The Worldwide People's Revolution!® Book 080. (See the Description on Amazon: because they Offer a ONE-MILLION-DOLLAR REWARD to anyone who can Prove our Selected King's Solutions to be WRong or Unworkable! Can you Beat that? Do you have all such Guaranteed Solutions? Does any Politician? Only our Selected King has those Provable Solutions: beCause God Blest him with them, which can be Proven in any Courtroom with Law and Order. ENJOY!)

[_] 40-081 — "Mexicans are more Intelligent than Americans!" (A Unique Challenge to all Americans and Mexicans!) By The Worldwide People's Revolution!® Book 081. {NOTE: The Remaining 275 Inspired Books by the Author of this Book may only be found in English, until we can get them Properly Translated into other Languages. Shame on you People who Killed him, who Broke his Heart with your Unbelief. May God have Mercy on your Poor Wretched Souls.} †§‡

[_] 40-081B — "¡Los Mexicanos son más Inteligentes que los Estadounidenses!" (¡Un Desafío Único para todos los Estadounidenses y Mexicanos!) By The Worldwide People's Revolution!® Book 082. {NOTA: Aquí está el primer Libro en Español, que puede no ser Perfecto; pero, es Perfectamente lo Suficientemente Bueno para Iluminar las Mentes de quien lo Estudia.}

[_] 40-082 — **"The Process of Making a RIGHTEOUS KING!"** (A Fascinating Autobiography of our Selected King!) By The Worldwide People's Revolution!® Book 082. {NOTE: He once had a 6,000-plus-page Autobiography, called: **"DIARRHEA of the Mind!"** which gave Details of his entire Life, since he was only 4 Years Old, when he had an Encounter with God, which has been Lost: beCause those Backup Disks became Obsolete, and were thus Trashed, along with the Obsolete Computer, which Costed 4,000-plus Dollars, along with the Hewlett-Packard Printer, which Costed another 4,000-plus Dollars, whose Antiquated Software would not Work with a Modern Computer, nor did Hewlett have an Updated Software Program for it: beCause they are Capitalist Scammers, who should be put Out of Business for Practicing Donald Trump Tactics! See: "The Nature of CAPITALISM!" (A List of the EVILS of CAPITALISM!) By The Worldwide People's Revolution!® Book 038.}

[_] 40-083 — **"Was Billy Graham Greatly Deceived?"** (Giving Honor to whom Honor is Due!) By The Worldwide People's Revolution!® Book 083. {NOTE: If you know a Grahamite, please Direct him or her to this Inspired Book, whereby he or she might be Converted to the Truths within it, and thus be Saved from Grahamite Perversions. Thank you in Advance. They will also Thank you for it: beCause they Suffer so Needlessly, when they should be Free, Healthy and Happy, like our Selected King, who has no Aches nor Pains, who used to Work Hard all Day long, and not be Weary, just like you can Reed in *the Book of Isaiah 40:31, NMV!*}

[_] 40-084 — **"The New MAGNIFIED Version of the Book of DEUTERONOMY!"** (The Understandable Version of Deuteronomy in Plain English!) Book 084. This is actually one of the Best Books within the entire Holy Bible, and also one of the Longest; but, do not allow that Fact to Deter you by any Means: beCause, "the Bigger Book is Normally a Better Book," which is True of a lot of Books, including all of the above Books: beCause it is the Nature of the Holy Spirit to get into Long-winded Sermons, you might say, which is WHY the Apostle Paul Preached until Midnight in *the Book of Acts,* until some Boy went to Sleep and Fell from a Window and Killed himself, whom the Apostle Paul Raised Up from the Dead and went on Preaching until the Dawn of the Day! And it is NOT Jewish Mythology! †§‡§§ {See: "The New MAGNIFIED Version of the Book of ACTS" for the Finest of Details, Book 063.}

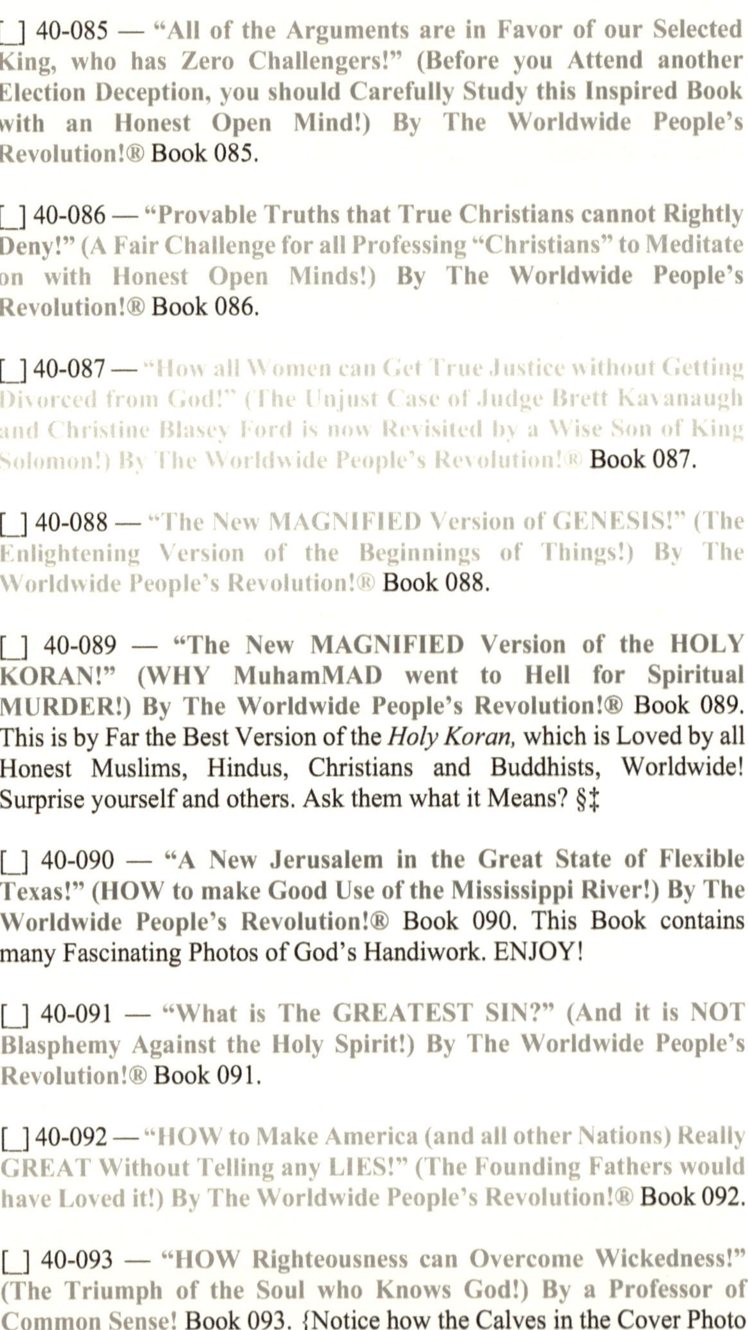

[_] 40-085 — "All of the Arguments are in Favor of our Selected King, who has Zero Challengers!" (Before you Attend another Election Deception, you should Carefully Study this Inspired Book with an Honest Open Mind!) By The Worldwide People's Revolution!® Book 085.

[_] 40-086 — "Provable Truths that True Christians cannot Rightly Deny!" (A Fair Challenge for all Professing "Christians" to Meditate on with Honest Open Minds!) By The Worldwide People's Revolution!® Book 086.

[_] 40-087 — "How all Women can Get True Justice without Getting Divorced from God!" (The Unjust Case of Judge Brett Kavanaugh and Christine Blasey Ford is now Revisited by a Wise Son of King Solomon!) By The Worldwide People's Revolution!® Book 087.

[_] 40-088 — "The New MAGNIFIED Version of GENESIS!" (The Enlightening Version of the Beginnings of Things!) By The Worldwide People's Revolution!® Book 088.

[_] 40-089 — "The New MAGNIFIED Version of the HOLY KORAN!" (WHY MuhamMAD went to Hell for Spiritual MURDER!) By The Worldwide People's Revolution!® Book 089. This is by Far the Best Version of the *Holy Koran,* which is Loved by all Honest Muslims, Hindus, Christians and Buddhists, Worldwide! Surprise yourself and others. Ask them what it Means? §‡

[_] 40-090 — "A New Jerusalem in the Great State of Flexible Texas!" (HOW to make Good Use of the Mississippi River!) By The Worldwide People's Revolution!® Book 090. This Book contains many Fascinating Photos of God's Handiwork. ENJOY!

[_] 40-091 — "What is The GREATEST SIN?" (And it is NOT Blasphemy Against the Holy Spirit!) By The Worldwide People's Revolution!® Book 091.

[_] 40-092 — "HOW to Make America (and all other Nations) Really GREAT Without Telling any LIES!" (The Founding Fathers would have Loved it!) By The Worldwide People's Revolution!® Book 092.

[_] 40-093 — "HOW Righteousness can Overcome Wickedness!" (The Triumph of the Soul who Knows God!) By a Professor of Common Sense! Book 093. {Notice how the Calves in the Cover Photo

Segregated themselves by their Colors, from Left to Right. God Guided them. †§‡}

[_] 40-094 — "Justifications for MAGNIFICATIONS!" (The Problem with Understanding a Complicated Contradictory Mutilated Unholy Bible!) Or: (The Problem with Inventing Lies that are too BIG to DIE!) By The Worldwide People's Revolution!® Book 094.

[_] 40-095 — "HOW to IDENTIFY God's Elected Ones!" (Are YOU one of the Elect?) By The Worldwide People's Revolution!® Book 095.

[_] 40-096 — "GOVERNMENT Versus Independence!" (How Much CONTROL Should a Government Have?") By The Worldwide People's Revolution!® Book 096.

[_] 40-097 — "C-SPAN-DEX!" (Your Filtered View of Bad Government!) By The Worldwide People's Revolution!® Book 097.

[_] 40-098 — "Profitable Swanky MULCHING ROCKS!" (30 Advantages for Using Swanky Mulching Rocks in an All-Mineral Organic Garden!) By The Worldwide People's Revolution!® Book 098. {Just Think, the School of Fools never Mentioned them, nor did the False Government, nor any of the False Churches: beCause they are Uneducated and Foolish.}

[_] 40-099 — "The Great ATOMIC NIGHTMARE!" (The Saddest Story in World History!) By The Great White Bald Eagle! Book 099. {NOTE: Let us Hope and Pray that no one ever has to Write this Book; but, if they Do, it should Spook the Devil Out of you!}

[_] 40-100 — "Our Selected King SPEAKS OUT!" (It is High Time for some Sane Person to get Total Control of this Insane World!) By The Worldwide People's Revolution!® Book 100!

[_] 40-101 — "What will you Do when the Rain STOPS?" (God's Last Resort to Save Mankind from his MADNESS!) By The Worldwide People's Revolution!® Book 101!

[_] 40-102 — "Beautiful Swanky Stone Dome Home COMPLEXES!" (HOW to Build SECURE Tax-proof, Insurance-proof, Self-air-conditioned, Paint-proof, Rot-proof, Termite-proof, Mouse-proof, Fireproof, Tornado-proof, Hurricane-proof, Thief-proof, and BOMB-PROOF Houses!) By The Worldwide People's Revolution!® Book 102.

[ ] 40-103 — "Royal Swanky Buffets!" (The Best Feasts in the Whole World!) By The Worldwide People's Revolution!® Book 103.

[ ] 40-104 — "101 Good Reasons and Great Advantages for Establishing a Righteous One-World Government!" (Government By the People, Of the People, and For the People!) By The Worldwide People's Revolution!® Book 104. This Book Suggests thousands of Good Reasons and Great Advantages. But, of course, you have to be Able to THINK, which seems to be something that Wicked Politicians cannot Do, or Refuse to Do; and neither can most Preachers and Teachers Do it. Therefore, this Inspired Book will Help them to Think and Remember.

[ ] 40-105 — "The New MAGNIFIED Version of the Book of REVELATION!" (The Understandable Version of the Most-Controversial Book in the Whole World!) By The Worldwide People's Revolution!® Book 105. This Proverbial "Bombshell" will be Published just before the Second Coming of Jesus Christ! Get your Seatbelts Fastened! Be Prepared for Radical Changes!

[ ] 40-106 — "The Naked Glory of Beautiful Mankind!" (1,000 Pages of Sheer Artistic BEAUTY!) By The Worldwide People's Revolution!® Book 106. (See Book 014B-02-09-T for the Explanation.)

[ ] 40-107 — "The Beautiful Faces of Holy Men!" (The very Best that God has to Offer!) By The Worldwide People's Revolution!® Book 107.

[ ] 40-108 — "The Worldwide People's Revolution!" (A Comprehensive Plan for Obtaining Worldwide Law, Order, Obedience, Peace and True Prosperity!) By The Worldwide People's Revolution!® Book 108.

[ ] 40-109 — "VOTE for The GOAT!" (The New Political Party that has Guaranteed Solutions for our Massive Problems!) By The Worldwide People's Revolution!® Book 109.

[_] 40-110 — "IMPORTANT THINGS that Should Have Been Written in the Holy Bible!" (A Special Challenge to all Professing Christians, Jews, Hindus, Muslims and Atheists!) **By The Irreverent Penname Scumbag!** Book 110.

[_] 40-111 — "Hosts of HOAXES Live In Under Around and Over the Little White OUTHOUSE!" (WHY Spiritually-Blind Cowardly-Americans are Hunkering Down in their Empty Root Cellars!) By The Irreverent Penname Oversight! Book 111.

[_] 40-112 — "Should Wives Obey their Husbands?" (OR, Should Husbands OBEY their Wives?) By The Irreverent Penname Mockingbird! Book 112.

[_] 40-113 — "Modern Deceived SLAVES!" (10 Simple Steps for Liberating ALL Modern Slaves, Worldwide, Including Yourself!) By Liberty and Justice for ALL! Book 113.

{NOTE: This List of Available Books will be Updated, Periodically, if we do not get Killed by some Lying Conniving Edomites!}

www.ingramcontent.com/pod-product-compliance
Lightning Source LLC
Chambersburg PA
CBHW021039160726
47994CB00006B/2633